CINEMANALYSIS:
LEARNING ABOUT PSYCHOLOGY THROUGH FILM

BY CRAIG POHLMAN AND JOSH JENSEN

CinemAnalysis:
Learning about Psychology Through Film

Copyright © 2015 by Hero House Publishing, Craig Pohlman, Ph.D. and Josh Jensen, LMFT

Hero House Publishing
6060 Piedmont Row Drive South
Suite 120
Charlotte, NC 28287
www.herohousepublishing.com

All Rights Reserved.

No part of this book may be printed or reproduced in any manor without the permission of the publisher.

Text design by Sara Caitlyn Deal; Cover design by Zach Brown

CinemAnalysis: Learning about psychology through film/ Pohlman, C. & Jensen, J.

ISBN-13: 978-0-9965467-1-3

Contents

Act I Sell Crazy Someplace Else: Cinematic Psychopathology
    Black Swan & Fight Club   9
    The Road & Children of Men   16
    Kill Bill: Volume 2 & Oldboy   21
    Match Point & In the Bedroom   25
    Sound of My Voice & Don Juan DeMarco   29
    Lars and the Real Girl & Harvey   33
    Melancholia & Take Shelter   37

Act II Family Thermo-Dynamics: Parents, Children, and Siblings on Screen
    Terms of Endearment & Postcards from the Edge   44
    Nothing in Common & Big Fish   48
    The Royal Tenenbaums & Little Miss Sunshine   52
    The Fabulous Baker Boys & Big Night   56
    You Can Count on Me & The Darjeeling Limited   59

Act III Through the Looking Glass: Identity on Film
    Up in the Air & The Accidental Tourist   64
    Sideways & Bunny and the Bull   68
    October Sky & Searching for Bobby Fischer   72
    Aliens & 28 Weeks Later   76
    The Incredibles & Hancock   80

Act IV Emotion Pictures: Romantic Relationships and Friendships
    Blue Valentine & Priceless   86
    Revolutionary Road & Scenes from a Marriage   90
    Say Anything & Garden State   95
    Waitress & Like Water for Chocolate   99
    Lost in Translation & The Station Agent   102

Act V Streaming Consciousness: Cognition & Perception in Movies
    Pan's Labyrinth & The Fall   106
    Inception & Waking Life   110
    Eternal Sunshine of the Spotless Mind & Vanilla Sky   115
    Pulp Fiction & Go   120

Act VI BioFlicks: Lifespan on Screen

 E.T. the Extra-Terrestrial & How to Train Your Dragon   126
 Where the Wild Things Are & Ferris Bueller's Day Off   131
 (500) Days of Summer & Annie Hall   136
 Before Sunrise, Before Sunset, & Before Midnight   139
 Bridesmaids & Jerry Maguire   143
 About Schmidt & The Visitor   148

PREFACE

We dig movies.

The inspiration for this book flows from that simple fact. The motion picture is the dominant art form of our time. It will be supplanted someday- it may even be happening right now with the rise of video games and interactive entertainment (television is staging a comeback, too). But movies rule the moment for a number of reasons. They immerse us in dynamic imagery, sound, and music. They provide escapism. They can evoke every emotion, from fear to joy to passion. They can stir our thoughts and pose consequential questions. But more than anything else, movies tell stories. And people love hearing (and telling) stories.

Several years ago we tapped into our affinity for film to blog about compelling double features. As we talked and thought about movies, we routinely found ourselves connecting them. "You know, *Bridesmaids* is a lot like *Jerry Maguire*," or "*Black Swan* is *Fight Club* staged to ballet." So we coined the term *separated-at-birth cinema* to capture the notion of two movies that share striking amounts of cinematic DNA. It was fun to pair movies, even when they spanned genres, decades, or tone (like *Harvey* and *Lars and the Real Girl*). Plus, the idea of a movie double feature is very nostalgic. Sadly, few theatres indulge in double features anymore. It soon may become entirely incumbent on film buffs to create double features in their home theatres (streaming services could help with that).

As mental health professionals (Craig- a neurodevelopmental psychologist, and Josh- a marriage and family therapist), it was only natural for psychological issues to surface in our musings on films. So then we found ourselves thinking about things like how the *Little Miss Sunshine* family really is a different generation of *The Royal*

Tenenbaums and that both films could be case studies on Murray Bowen's theory of differentiation. Using movies to illustrate psychological principles is well-trodden ground, especially with regard to psychopathology. There also are books out there that cover how to view movies as part of therapy.

But we're offering something unique. First, presenting our suggestions for double features infuses a bit of whimsy in the proceedings. We want this book to be an accessible introduction to some foundational content about psychology. Second, embedding ideas within a double feature, as opposed to individual films, broadens our capacity to make connections and explore nuances. For instance, connecting *E.T. The Extra-Terrestrial* with *How to Train Your Dragon* allows us to touch on all three of Baumrind's parenting styles. Third, we run a gamut with our content, drawing on theory, research, and our clinical experience (on issues such as relationships, grief, parenting, and self-esteem). This book is much more than an exercise in diagnostic character study.

We organized the book in 6 parts (or "Acts"), each containing several double features with a common psychological thread, be it psychopathology, relationships, or the lifespan. Although we tried to include a representative sample of topics in each Act (like stages of development in the lifespan act), we know we didn't come close to an exhaustive list of all relevant psychological material related to our movie choices. But we do believe our film selections are some of the best out there. This is our list of top films, all paired up according to shared cinematic DNA and illustrating psychological themes.

Finally, we should add that as much as we love movies, we *hate* spoilers. Experiencing something fresh, unexpected, or even shocking when watching a movie is one of things that makes it special. We have tried to avoid spoilers at every turn, but be forewarned that we had to include some in order to make certain points. So please accept our apology up front.

   Roll camera . . .

Act I
Sell Crazy Someplace Else:
Cinematic Psychopathology

Black Swan (2010) & Fight Club (1999)

All of us want control. And why shouldn't we? After all, the world can be a dangerous and painful place if we don't assert our will over it. But at what point does our control get in the way? These two films depict characters working out their troubled relationships with control; reaping the benefits of enlightenment, but paying the toll with their bodies and minds.

When the Walls Come Crumbling Down

Black Swan is a mind-bending thriller following the story of Nina, a perfectionist ballet dancer who wants nothing more than to be cast as the lead role, the Swan Queen, which is a dual role as the Black Swan and the White Swan. Soon after this dream is realized, she is congratulated on her portrayal of the White Swan, but is told repeatedly that she must let go of her perfectionist habits and become the more devious and self-destructive Black Swan. Inspiration for becoming the Black Swan comes from a fellow dancer and newcomer, Lilly. Lilly is the perfect Black Swan and in this way, Nina's competition. As the story unfolds, Nina becomes so immersed in her roles and the dynamics of those around her that she (like the audience) is unable to decipher reality from fantasy as her hallucinations become more bizarre and horrific.

Fight Club also keeps the audience guessing about what is reality and what is fantasy. An unlikely friendship develops between the nameless narrator of the story (we'll refer to him here as "Jack") and Tyler Durden, who are both discontented with society and the meaning of manhood in the modern world. What do they do about it? Start an underground club where guys beat each other's faces in, obviously. Even though the philosophy might sound like a plug for anarchy (and at times it is), this film also makes some profound statements about masculinity (and emasculation), as well as the existential crisis of upward mobility.

In addition to the parallel of hallucinations, these films show main characters struggling with expectations of gender roles and characters who are willing to damage (or even destroy) their bodies for the sake of transcendence. What's more, they both question the meaning of perfection and self-improvement. While Nina's instructor tells her, "Perfection is not just about control. It's also about letting go," Tyler Durden tells Jack to, "Just let go!" of the wheel of a moving car. Both films end with tragedy, softened perhaps by some degree of inspiration. Jack has to shoot himself in the head in order to put an end to Tyler's reign of havoc. Jack's willingness to kill himself kills Tyler. Jack survives and finally may be able to move forward with his life as he reaches for the hand of Marla and says "you've met me at a very strange time in my life." Nina also has to kill her inner demon by stabbing herself with a broken mirror during the final acts of her show. This act of letting go eventually proves fatal but not before it produces the most spectacular applause from the ballet audience. She is also mesmerized by being part of this perfect moment as she takes her last breath.

> **BLACK SWAN**
>
> **Directed by**
> Darren Aronofsky
>
> **Cast**
> Natalie Portman as Nin Sayers, Mila Kunis as Lily, Vincent Cassel as Thomas Leroy, Barbara Hershey as Erica Sayers, Winona Ryder as Beth Macintyre
>
> **Oscar Wins**
> Best Performance by an Actress in a Leading Role (Natalie Portman)
>
> **Oscar Nominations**
> Best Motion Picture of the Year
> Best Achievement in Directing
> Best Achievement in Cinematography
> Best Achievement in Film Editing
>
> **Golden Globe Wins**
> Best Performance by an Actress in a Motion Picture (Natalie Portman)
>
> **Metascore: 79**

Destructive Perfectionism

Psychosis is one of the most fascinating, yet extremely painful, human experiences. It is defined by a loss of contact with reality which includes delusions (false beliefs) and/or hallucinations (seeing, hearing, smelling or feeling things that are not there).[1] The term psychosis can encompass many illnesses such as schizophrenia, delusional disorder, and dementia. Psychosis, and several symptoms of schizophrenia and DID (Dissociative Identity Order) – formerly known as MPD (Multiple Personality Disorder), accurately describe some of what is depicted in *Fight Club* and *Black* Swan; however, no single diagnosis can explain all of what we see in Nina or Tyler/Jack.

Just as the disclaimer "based on actual events" is used for historical fiction, these films might well adopt the disclaimer "based on actual symptoms of real disorders." Both movies portray a hodgepodge of symptoms that do exist, but they would likely follow a more predictable trajectory. Schizophrenics tend to become more mentally disorganized (not thinking coherently) and disconnected from themselves and others (in other words, "losing it"). Likewise, those with anxiety and impulse control disorders can become more consumed with their anxiety reducing rituals. So we would expect Nina's and Jack's symptoms to become pronounced and debilitating rather than developing into new symptoms. When you have a head cold, you often have the symptoms of a runny nose, cough, or sore throat but if you started noticing a rash on your skin, you would be right to assume that this symptom was related to a separate condition.

In *Black Swan* Nina is often seen exercising extreme restraint in her eating, like causing herself to throw up in the bathroom. She's always worried about her performance. She excessively picks at her scabs, washes her hands, and perfectly performs rituals of dressing and lining up her make-up. These symptoms point toward disorders such as anorexia, bulimia, anxiety, and obsessive-compulsive disorder (OCD). All of these disorders and their associated cluster of anxiety-related symptoms are likely to co-occur.[2] But OCD, in particular, is considered unrelated to, and therefore more unlikely to co-occur with, her later symptoms of hallucinations. An individual with OCD feels compelled to behave in ways that soothe their anxiety even if they know the act is irrational. Because the actions are irrational, OCD is often misdiagnosed as schizophrenia; differentiating intrusive thoughts of OCD and hallucinations of schizophrenia can be quite difficult for the clinician due to how similar each might be described by the client. But they are very different experiences.[3]

In *Fight Club* Jack hallucinates that Tyler is his new friend. He later realizes that actually he is Tyler and he only is imaging himself observing Tyler. His auditory and visual hallucinations look a lot like schizophrenia but this disorder (contrary to popular usage) is quite distinct from DID. A person with DID understands himself as having "alternates," or distinct personalities that occupy the same body. So DID is about delusions (or false beliefs) rather than hallucinations.[4] In many cases of DID the person afflicted is a survivor of some kind of trauma, such as sexual abuse, and alternates are thought to insulate the person from a perceived threat.[5] There is even debate as to whether DID should be considered psychosis. Many researchers and clinicians believe it more accurately belongs in the

> **FIGHT CLUB**
>
> **Directed by**
> David Fincher
>
> **Cast**
> Edward Norton as Jack, Brad Pitt as Tyler Durden, Helena Bonham Carter as Marla Singer, Meat Loaf as Robert 'Bob' Paulsen, Zach Grenier as Richard Chesler
>
> **Oscar Nominations**
> Best Effects, Sound Effects Editing
>
> **Metascore: 66**

category of an anxiety disorder because the person has been so traumatized that they use alternates as defense mechanisms to avoid perceived threats. This etiology doesn't seem to hold up from what we know of Jack/Tyler. The film gives no hint that Jack was once a victim of sexual abuse nor does his alternate, Tyler, seem to serve as a protective force against sexually vulnerable situations.

In both films characters are pushed, or push themselves, to such extremes of existential angst that they "snap." Certainly the emotional turmoil could lead many to "lose it," but the symptoms that follow would likely chart a more predictable course. For instance, Nina's OCD symptoms could likely become more extreme to the point that she spends hours and hours performing anxiety reducing rituals. Likewise, Jack might become increasingly disorganized in his attempts to plan attacks or lead his army of anarchists. In both case, if their mental illnesses really were ramping up, we would likely see much more nonfunctional versions of them at the ends of their stories.

Filmmakers are obligated to be faithful to a narrative rather than a well-articulated case study on psychopathology. It might be helpful to equate "psychological drama" to psychology the way we do to with "science fiction" and science. When science fiction is done well, we are inspired towards adventure and "what ifs?" Likewise, dramas like *Black Swan* and *Fight Club* can improve our understanding of psychological disorders and deepen our empathy for the people who have them.

Notes

[1] Berger, F.K. (2012). *Psychosis.* PubMed Health A.D.A.M Medical Encyclopedia. Retrieved from http://www.ncbi.nlm.nih.gov/pubmed-health/PMH0002520/

[2] Kaye, W.H., Bulik, C.M., Thornton, L., Barbarich, N., & Masters, K.

(2004). Comorbidity of anxiety disorders with anorexia and bulimia nervosa. *American Journal of Psychiatry, 161,* 2215–2221.

[3] Veale, D., Freeston, M., Krebs, G., Heyman, I., Salkovskis, P. (2013) Risk assessment and management in obsessive-compulsive disorder. *Advances in Psychiatric Treatment, 15* (5), 332-342. doi: 10.1192/apt.bp.107.004705

[4] Tartakovsky, M. (2011). *Dispelling Myths about Dissociative Identity Disorder.* Retrieved from http://psychcentral.com/lib/2011/dispelling-myths-about-dissociative-identity-disorder/

[5] Ross, C.A. (1997). *Dissociative identity disorder: Diagnosis, clinical features, and treatment of multiple personality (2nd ed.).* New York: Wiley.

The Road (2009) & Children of Men (2006)

Apocalyptic cinema is like science-fiction's melodramatic sibling. While sci-fi takes us beyond life as we know it, apocalyptic narratives deconstruct our paradigm of civilization, stripping human interactions to the basest of instinctive drives. These next films remove another layer of our preconceived constructs and provide a raw glimpse at humanity, including grief and depression.

Now Apocalypse

The Road depicts a father and son, only referred to as "the Man" and "the Boy." The details of the recent past are equally non-descriptive. A cataclysmic disaster has turned the world cold, dark, and full of ash to the point that there are no living plants or animals. Most of the few human survivors have resorted to cannibalism as a means to live just a little longer. It is through these ruthless villains and the treacherous terrain that the Man and Boy must travel in the hope that the southern coast might sustain some life. As the odds of survival are stacked so high against them, the Man contemplates the futility of their striving. Their love for each other gives them every reason but they just don't have the means. So why keep struggling in the face of the inevitable? Because as the Man assures the Boy (and maybe himself), "This is what the good guys do. They keep trying. They don't give up."

> **The Road**
>
> **Directed by**
> John Hilcoat
>
> **Cast**
> Viggo Mortensen as Man, Kodi Smit-McPhee as Boy, Robert Duvall as Old Man, Guy Pearce as Veteran, Molly Parker as Motherly Woman, Charlize Theron as Woman, Michael K. Williams as Thief
>
> **Metascore: 64**

Children of Men is set in the not-too-distant future of 2027 where human beings face global extinction. The pandemic isn't disease, nuclear war, or a giant meteor, but something much more subtle- infertility. The youngest person is now 18 and the world is falling apart- not because children are needed to maintain order, but because without them, what's the point? Anger is the dominant mood and anarchy is the dominant political persuasion. The story follows a disillusioned hero, Theo, as he tries to help a young woman, Kee, get to the coast in hopes that she holds the key to halting human extinction.

Both films show the world as we know it dying with a whimper rather than a bang. They also show lone heroes striving to get to the sea as their last desperate attempt at salvation. While the Man and Boy in *The Road* hope for the meager basics of survival in an uninhabitable world, Theo and Kee in *Children of Men* hope for a reason to survive in a world devoid of a meaningful future.

Grief or Belief

Grief and depression have many overlapping symptoms and yet should be understood as quite different experiences. *The Road* and *Children of Men* highlight the differences between the two. *The Road* depicts grief. The Man and the Boy are *grieving* over the death of their world and even present some signs of what Kübler-Ross called the 5 stages of grief[1]:

1. denial and isolation
2. anger
3. bargaining
4. depression
5. acceptance

For example, the Man and Boy are in denial that the

world isn't dead but is alive somewhere farther south. Unlike severe cases of depression, they believe that their life is worth living, if only they could find the resources to sustain it. They do find resources like food and shelter, albeit briefly. It is at these points that their despair is temporarily lifted. In her classic work on grief, *Nothing Was the Same*, renowned clinical psychologist Kay Jamison commented that the capacity to be consoled is what distinguishes grief and depression.[2]

Depression is personified in *Children of Men* when Theo asks the question, "What's the point?" Depression is not simply the product of bad circumstances, it is the *perceived* loss of meaning and value in one's life. Theo and Kee believe that their world will have no value or meaning if there are no more children. Short of this, they cannot be consoled. By contrast, even though their world would still be in shambles should a baby is born, it would provide them with a reason or "point" to their existence.

> **CHILDREN OF MEN**
>
> **Directed by**
> Alfonso Cuarón
>
> **Cast**
> Clive Owen as Theo Faron, Michael Caine as Jasper, Chiwetel Ejiofor as Luke, Juan Gabriel Yacuzzi as Baby Diego, Julianne Moore as Julian
>
> **Oscar Nominations**
> Best Achievement in Cinematography
> Best Achievement in Film Editing
> Best Writing, Adapted Screenplay
>
> **Metascore: 84**

One of the controversial changes from the DSM-IV to DSM-5 was how it differentiates grief and depression. The DSM-IV stipulated that diagnosing Major Depressive Disorder (MDD) was inappropriate during the first 2 months of bereavement.[3] By contrast, authors of the DSM-5 removed this "bereavement exclusion" with the rationale that this helps prevent overlooking depression and opens the possibility of co-occurring grief and depression. Because of these changes, the APA highlighted some of the key differences between depression and grief symptoms[4]:

- "In grief, painful feelings come in waves, often intermixed with positive memories of the deceased; in depression, mood and ideation are almost constantly negative.

- In grief, self-esteem is usually preserved; in MDD, corrosive feeling of worthlessness and self-loathing are common.

- While many believe that some form of depression is a normal consequence of bereavement, MDD should not be diagnosed in the context of bereavement since diagnosis would incorrectly label a normal process as a disorder."

As far as we know, Theo doesn't have diminished self-worth, but ideation and a consistent, negative mood does seem to be present, in contrast to the Man and Boy who seem to experience temporary reprieve. Even though Kee may be able to bring about the end of infertility, we don't see much change in Theo's mood. If anything, he might jump from depression to anxiety when he realizes that human life might be sustained. One thing is clear: tremendous sadness and withdrawal is present for all of the protagonists. But categorizing emotional states depends greatly on the context.

Notes

[1] Kübler-Ross, E. (1969). *On death and dying.* Toronto, Canada: Macmillan.

[2] Jamison, K. (2009). *Nothing was the same: A memoir.* New York: First Vintage Books Edition.

[3] American Psychiatric Association. (2000). *Diagnostic and statistical manual of mental disorders* (4th ed., text rev.). Washington, DC: Author.

[4] American Psychiatric Association. (2013). *Diagnostic and statistical manual of mental disorders* (5th ed.). Washington, DC: Author.

KILL BILL: VOLUME 2 (2004) & OLDBOY (2003)

Sometimes a good way to further understand health is to study pathology. So what motivates a person to snap and go on a rampage? This chapter explores the burning desire for revenge when it is motivated by intense grief and shame.

A Dish Best Served Cold

Kill Bill is Quentin Tarantino's 2-part saga of Beatrix Kiddo, a woman who is bent on killing her eponymous former lover and criminal kingpin. *Volume 2* provides the back-story of how Beatrix (aka, "the Bride") was groomed to become an assassin, fell in love with Bill, and later abandoned her life of crime. Bill was not very happy with her career change and tried to kill her, instead putting her in a coma. The (supposed) death of her unborn child is the principal motivator for her to kill Bill at any cost (even though he's the father). Eventually she learns that her child is, in fact, alive and in the care of Bill. In rediscovering the love for her child, the child's love for her father, and the duality of tenderness and brutality in Bill, the Bride's motivations for revenge become much more complicated.

> **KILL BILL: VOLUME 2**
>
> **Directed by**
> Quentin Tarantino
>
> **Cast**
> Uma Thurman as Beatrix Kiddo, Micheal Madsen as Budd, Daryl Hannah as Elle Driver, David Carradine as Bill, Vivica Fox as Vernita Green, Ambrosia Kelly as Nikki, Lucy Liu as O-Renn Ishii, Samuel L. Jackson as Rufus
>
> **Metascore: 83**

At the outset of *Oldboy*, Dea-su is locked in a cell for 15 years without any human contact and without any knowledge of why he is being punished. He becomes both overwhelmed with guilt (questioning over and over which of his sins are responsible for his predicament) and consumed with vengeance against his captors. He discovers that there is a man solely responsible, and he too is motivated by revenge. The two adversaries calculate what would cause the other the most suffering because killing each other is simply not enough. As the stakes are raised higher and higher it becomes clear that vengeance is the true villain in the story.

Pain for My Shame

Humans are known for perpetuating cycles of violence that can go beyond a lifetime and run through generations. In both of these films, the actions taken by either party (good guy or bad guy) can be enormously sinister. But that doesn't mean those perpetuating the pattern are inherently evil. We derive our sense of justice by what we see as fair or balanced. Reciprocity is important in maintaining order in society and in relationships. However, when a person is overcome by their subjective experience of inflicted pain, a shift from justice to revenge happens when the repayment is disproportionate to the offense.[1] This occurs in *Kill Bill* when Bill sends an assassin to kill Beatrix because he is sure she has cheated on him (when, in fact, it is his baby she is carrying). Beatrix is sure that Bill has killed her unborn child (when, in fact, he has taken tremendous care of her ever since she was born). Likewise, Dea-su and his nemesis, Mr. Han, wreak enormous havoc in pursuit of repayment for their intensely personal injuries, but no payback is sufficient and revenge never fully satisfies.

OLDBOY

Directed by
Chan-wook Park

Cast
Min-sik Choi as Dae-su Oh, Ji-tae Yu as Woo-jin Lee, Hye-jeong Kang as Mi-do

Metascore: 74

Research has identified that a person's experience of shame and grief is highly correlated with a tendency towards revenge.[2] Certainly, Bill felt shamed by what he thought was Beatrix's betrayal, and Beatrix was motivated out of grief. This pattern also fits with Dea-su and Mr. Han, with both having a deep sense of shame that they perceive (rightly or not) that the other had inflicted. Both stories end with tragedy, *Oldboy* more so than *Kill Bill*. The obvious lesson is that the destructive force of revenge leads to more harm than good for both recipient and aggressor. It is a no brainer that resentment, bitterness, and revenge are catastrophic to the fabric of a society because the abuse never ends. What is equally true, but less obvious, is that revenge is also enormously costly to the perpetrator's psyche. Research has shown various forms of mental illness such as PTSD and depression are significantly more common in individuals who are unforgiving.[3] Some researchers argue that revenge and forgiveness both serve a purpose in human history and biology. For ancient humans, revenge served the role of reciprocity in providing checks and balances for offenses; however, humans have flourished by combining this need for reciprocity with our ability to cooperate, and cooperation is impossible without tolerance of others' mistakes.[4] Without forgiveness, our mistakes produce a constant cycle of retribution that directly undermines our cooperation. Not only do we need forgiveness to keep our society together, McCullough believes it is so common that it often goes unnoticed: "In daily life, forgiveness is more often like a Band-Aid on a scrape and at first glance perhaps only slightly more interesting. But, of course, uninteresting doesn't mean unimportant".[5] We forgive our children constantly for drawing with crayons on the walls or elbowing us in the jaw. The reason we may not label this everyday response as forgiveness could be due to the misunderstanding that forgiving is some kind of heroic act that only exceptional humans manage to accomplish. Since this ability is so important to our personal and social health, it's encouraging to hear that it might be more available to each of us then we think.

So now that we've heard this good news, the next chapter offers more bad news. Just as our capacity to heal interpersonally is closer than we might think, so is our capacity towards violence.

Notes

[1] Rosenbaum, T. (2001). Eye for an eye: The case for revenge. *The Chronicle Review.* Retrieved from http://chronicle.com/article/The-Case-for-Revenge/138155/

[2] Bloom, S. L. (2001). Commentary: reflections on the desire for revenge. *Journal of Emotional Abuse, 2,* 61-94.

[3] Kaminer, D., Stein, D.J., Mbanga, I., & Zungu-Dirwayi, N. (2001). The Truth and Reconciliation Commission in South Africa: Relation to psychiatric status and forgiveness among survivors of human rights abuses. *British Journal of Psychiatry, 178,* 373-377.

[4] Abkowitz, M. & McCullough, M. (2008). *Beyond Revenge: The Evolution of the Forgiveness Instinct.* San Francisco: Jossey-Bass.

[5] Tippit, K. & McCullough, M. (2012). *Getting Revenge and Forgiveness* [Audio podcast]. Retrieved from http://www.onbeing.org/program/getting-revenge-and-forgiveness/transcript/4575

Match Point (2005) & In the Bedroom (2001)

With all the mayhem happening around the world (or down the street), most people would like to think that they are not capable of committing atrocities. But humans are animals, after all, and circumstances can bring out the animal in just about anybody. This double feature won't be uplifting, but it'll make up for it with suspense and insight into the nether corners of human nature. Let's take a look at how ordinary people can be pushed to murderous extremes.

Crazy is as Crazy Does

Match Point is a rare dramatic thriller in director Woody Allen's filmography. Chris is a former tennis pro who would like to build a better life for himself in London. He gets involved with the charming rich girl Chloe, who becomes his meal ticket. However, he becomes obsessed with Nola, the American girlfriend of Chloe's brother. Chris marries Chloe and then starts a scorching affair with Nola. When he realizes his infidelity could not only cost him his marriage, but also his upper-crust lifestyle, he hatches a diabolical plan to murder Nola and their unborn child.

Match Point is one of those movies with a protagonist that you may find yourself pulling for, despite the cruelty and cold-bloodedness. *In the Bedroom* offers more sympathetic characters also pressed to homicide. Matt and Ruth lose their son, Frank, when he gets caught in the crossfire of a domestic dispute between his girlfriend, Natalie, and her estranged husband, Richard. Due to narrow eyewitness testimony and limited ballistic evidence, Richard gets off easy. So Matt and Ruth take matters into their own hands, and their hands get bloody. While *Match Point* plays like a methodically-paced thriller, *In the Bedroom* is a mood-drenched tragedy.

Violent Outliers

So why, or how, do people become murderers? Research has identified some personality traits that put individuals at risk for violence, even against loved ones. These traits include self-centeredness[1] and lack of emotional regulation.[2] More specifically, research has suggested that the risk of violence can be viewed along four fundamental personality dimensions: 1) impulse control, 2) affect regulation, 3) narcissism, and 4) paranoid thinking.[3]

These factors seem to apply more to Chris (*Match Point*) than Matt and Ruth (*In the Bedroom*). Chris shows plenty of signs of egoism, and his emotions are all over the map in terms of affection for his wife and lust for his lover. But while he may be impulsive sexually, his methodical and diabolical plotting of Nola's murder is anything but impulsive (an insanity defense would be a tough sell). He also could be viewed as a sociopath, or a person with anti-social personality disorder: a long-standing pattern of thought and behavior that significantly deviates from the individual's cultural norms, and is pervasive and rigid, manifesting itself in extreme antisocial attitudes and behavior and a lack of conscience.[4] This last attribute is huge, as Chris goes so far as to characterize the killing of his unborn child as acceptable collater-

> **MATCH POINT**
>
> **Directed by**
> Woody Allen
>
> **Cast**
> Jonathan Rhys Meyers as Chris Wilton, Scarlett Johansson as Nola Rice, Matthew Goode as Tom Hewett, Emily Mortimer as Chloe Hewett Wilton, Alexander Armstrong as Mr. Townsend
>
> **Oscar Nominations**
> Best Writing, Original Screenplay
>
> **Metascore: 72**

al damage in wartime.

Matt and Ruth's motives are just as deadly, but not so unseemly. They are out for justice, having seen their son's murderer get an unacceptably light sentence. Vigilantism is hardly a higher calling, but in their circumstances the psychopathology is less extreme. *In the Bedroom* has some interesting moments in which Matt and Ruth get lost in their thoughts or lash out at others, including Natalie. So affect regulation (controlling emotions, including responses to emotions) would be the factor that best applies to them- not so much for narcissism and paranoia. Impulse control? Like Chris in *Match Point*, Matt and Ruth carry out their plan in a disturbingly calm and calculating manner (a portion of which while listening to a Boston Red Sox game on a car radio). The biggest rule-out for sociopathy for them may be conscience. To be sure, they execute their son's killer and we never see them shed a tear. But in the immediate aftermath we do see them start to bear the weight of what they have done.

> **IN THE BEDROOM**
>
> **Directed by**
> Todd Field
>
> **Cast**
> Tom Wilkinson as Matt Fowler, Sissy Spacek as Ruth Fowler, Nick Stahl as Frank Fowler, Marisa Tomei as Natalie Strout, William Mapother as Richard Strout
>
> **Oscar Nominations**
> Best Picture
> Best Actor in a Leading Role (Tom Wilkinson)
> Best Actress in a Leading Role (Sissy Spacek)
> Best Actress in a Supporting Role (Marisa Tomei)
>
> **Golden Globe Wins**
> Best Performance by an Actress in a Motion Picture – Drama (Sissy Spacek)
>
> **Metascore: 86**

Notes

[1] Dean, K. E., & Malamuth, N. M. (1997). Characteristics of men who aggress sexually and of men who imagine aggressing: Risk and

moderating variables. *Journal of Personality and Social Psychology, 72*, 449–455.

[2] McNulty, J. K., & Hellmuth, J. C. (2008). Emotion regulation and intimate partner violence in newlyweds. *Journal of Family Psychology, 22*, 794–797.

[3] Nestor, P.G. (2002). Mental disorder and violence: Personality dimensions and clinical features. *American Journal of Psychiatry, 159*, 1973-1778.

[4] American Psychiatric Association (2013). *Diagnostic and statistical manual of mental disorders* (5th ed.). Washington, DC: Author.

Sound of My Voice (2011) & Don Juan DeMarco (1994)

Previous chapters have addressed how psychological resources and liabilities exist in everyone. The next cinematic pairing examines traits that exist in benevolent and malevolent leaders. These two films remind us to never underestimate the power of a charismatic personality.

After Me

In *Sound of My Voice,* Maggie is a cult leader who claims to be from the year 2054. Despite her inability to authenticate her temporal immigration, she amasses a small group of very loyal followers who are eager to learn the disciplines of mind and body needed to survive an impending, Armageddon-like "civil war." The story is told through the eyes of Peter and Lorna, a couple who pretend to be loyal followers in hopes that they can document and expose the absurdity of cult followings. But the deeper Peter and Lorna go to prove their loyalty, the more they are compelled by Maggie's magnetism. As the film progresses, what is true becomes less and less clear.

Don Juan DeMarco is about the eponymous "greatest lover in the world." Because of his outlandish assertions and an attempted suicide, he is admitted into a psychiatric hospital for a 10-day evaluation by psychiatrist Jack Mickler. Although Jack is about to retire, he and the rest of his staff take special interest in Don Juan's stories. As the time approaches for Jack to make a recommendation about what should be done with his young patient, Jack seems less interested in challenging delusions and more interested in making changes in his own life. Crazy or not, Jack needs what Don Juan has in order to revive the passionless relationship with his wife, Marilyn.

At the core, both movies are about human relationships, seduction, and enlightenment. One way to push beyond the limitations of our perspectives is by observing characters who are crazy, alien, or supernatural. Both films challenge assumptions about what is possible by presenting characters with impossible claims who offer something vital (and possible) that other characters are missing.

What Do Gandhi and Hitler Have in Common?

Charisma. Both Maggie and Don Juan have the ability to mesmerize followers who are willing to submit to their guidance and authority. And while it might be argued that they didn't cause a great deal of harm to others, other influential business, political, and religious leaders have been known to entrance their followers to the point of atrocities. Jim Jones is perhaps the best known cult leader in recent history. In 1978 he led 909 of his followers to commit suicide. This horrific event sent social psychologists scrambling to identify what enables a person to seduce others to such an extreme.

A narcissistic personality type is at the top of the list for these leaders. Not only do they have the unwavering confidence in themselves and their decisions, but they feed off of situations where they can use and manipulate others for their own gain.[1] But why on earth are others drawn to this? In cult followings a "Mirror-hungry" personality draws in the "Ideal-hungry"

> **SOUND OF MY VOICE**
>
> **Directed by**
> Zal Batmanglij
>
> **Cast**
> Christopher Denham as Peter Aitken, Nicole Vicius as Lorna Michaelson, Brit Marling as Maggie, Davenia McFadden as Carol Briggs
>
> **Metascore: 67**

personality (Post, 1986). A match is made when a leader who sees himself as possessing god-like authority recruits needy followers who eagerly seek a god to serve. In other words, the leader craves worship and the followers crave something to worship.

Both Don Juan and Maggie have a grandiose sense of who they are. They also speak of ideals that our protagonists seem to crave. Dr. Mickler realizes how much he has neglected the sensual aspects of his wife (and he wants to get his groove back). He's even willing to sacrifice some of his professional credibility and be a disciple of Don. Maggie claims to be from the future and has secret knowledge about surviving the impending disaster. It seems her followers crave security and are willing to ritualistically cleanse themselves of all "contaminants" like she demands. Peter begins his involvement as a skeptic because he isn't interested in buying the security she is selling; however, Maggie draws out an intense emotional catharsis that he was previously unable to achieve. He finds that he too needs this and consequently becomes more devoted to Maggie.

> **DON JUAN DEMARCO**
>
> **Directed by**
> Jeremy Leven
>
> **Cast**
> Marlon Brando as Dr. Jack Mickler, Johnny Depp as Don Juan, Faye Dunaway as Marliyn Mickler, Géraldine Pailhas as Doña Ana, Bob Dishy as Dr. Paul Showalter
>
> **Oscar Nominations**
> Best Music, Original Song "Have You Ever Really Loved a Woman"
>
> **Metascore: 63**

Experts on evil like Dr. Philip Zimbardo point out that one of the hallmarks of the destructive charismatic leader is the polarization of followers with outside groups, and creating an "us vs. them" mentality.[2] Once this is achieved, the leader can more easily manipulate followers by threatening or carrying out various forms of non-acceptance, ridicule, or rejection by the primary group for failing to comply with the leader's demands.[3] For the most part, Maggie and Don Juan don't go this far, but the protagonists in their fold do walk a fine line between gaining enlightenment and being duped.

Notes

[1] Rosenthal, S.A. & Pittinsky, T.L. (2006). Narcissistic leadership. *The Leadership Quarterly, 17*, 617-633.

[2] Post, J.M. (1986). Narcissism and the charismatic leader-follower relationship. *Political Psychology, 7*, 675-688.

[3] Zimbardo, P. & Andersen, S. (1993). Understanding mind control: Exotic and mundane mental manipulations. In M. Langone (Ed.), *Recovery from Cults: Help for Victims of Psychological and Spiritual Abuse* (pp. 104-125). New York: Norton.

LARS AND THE REAL GIRL (2007) & HARVEY (1950)

To this point we've covered a lot of down-beat topics like psychosis, grieving, depression, revenge, and manipulation. Feel-good movies that provide insight about psychopathology are rare, but the tandem featured in this chapter pull this off with elegance and depth. In fact, these films embody some of the core tenants of positive psychology, an important movement within the field.

You're Never Too Old to Have an Imaginary Friend

Pairing films from disparage eras enables comparing and contrasting not only artistic perspectives, but also cultural mindsets. These two films each contain a story of a socially isolated man with an imaginary friend and how each of their respective communities navigate their delusions.

Lars and the Real Girl begins with a quiet glimpse into the world of a socially anxious man named Lars. He is painfully awkward and avoidant of others, especially those who show any interest in pulling him out of his shell, including his brother and sister-in-law. He drops a bomb when he tells them he has a new girlfriend named Bianca. They met over the Internet (of course), she doesn't speak English (naturally), she's in a wheelchair (okay), and ... she is an "anatomically correct" plastic doll (boom). And one more thing- Lars does not seem to be aware of this last part (BOOM). He talks about her and treats her like a person. With Bianca in his life he starts to emerge from his shell. Others in the small town are dismayed and assume he must be crazy (or a pervert). But they come to realize that maybe Lars' delusions serve a very real purpose in giving him the courage to connect with others. Eventually the community decides that if they want to help Lars, they will have to treat Bianca as if she was real. Folks then display affection between each other through Bianca in remarkable and heartwarming ways.

In *Harvey*, we meet Elwood P. Dowd who, unlike Lars, is not socially phobic; on the contrary, he a social outcast but "oh, so pleasant." But in the fashion of Lars, Elwood can't help but introduce everyone to his best friend, who happens to be an invisible 6' 3 (& ½)" rabbit named Harvey. The comedy and action of the story begin when we meet Elwood's sister Vetta, who prides herself as a lady of "society." She states that she is unable to bear the shame that is brought by Elwood's preposterous behaviors; therefore, she is determined to commit him to a sanatorium (otherwise known as the "loony bin"). On arrival, Vetta is exasperated and Elwood is his normal, cheerful self. Initially, the attending doctor miscalculates and assumes that Vetta is the crazy one and Elwood is free to go. The mistake is later realized but the rest of the film continually reassesses the question of whether something is wrong with Elwood or with everyone else? The ending scenes have some profound dialogue from Elwood that, despite their skepticism, inspires a few psychiatric doctors and nurses to see that he has discovered a secret to living a more graceful life. He is so eloquent that he has a similar effect on the audience.

> **LARS AND THE REAL GIRL**
>
> **Directed by**
> Craig Gillespie
>
> **Cast**
> Ryan Gosling as Lars Lindstrom, Emily Mortimer as Karin, Paul Schneider as Gus, R.D. Reid as Reverend Bock, Kelli Garner as Margo, Patricia Clarkson as Dagmar
>
> **Oscar Nominations**
> Best Writing, Original Screenplay
>
> **Metascore: 70**

Adaptive Pathology

Psychosis is one of the most serious and terrifying forms of mental illness. Filmmakers are well aware of the common fear of "going crazy" and often capitalize on it. But the writers of these two films attempt to do something more than scare audiences: they ask what happens when the illness does not impair the individual. In the case of both Lars and Elwood, their delusions are, in a certain regard, helpful. Lars needed the idea of a supportive girlfriend like Bianca to overcome his social anxiety and better connect with others. Once he is integrated into the community Bianca becomes unnecessary and she "dies." Elwood used to live his life being what he referred to as "oh, so smart," but eventually found this mode inferior to being "oh, so pleasant." Elwood greets strangers at his local bar with intentionality. He doesn't just want to impress them and thereby get ahead in life; he wants to give them a sense of enlightenment. He knows that "no one brings anything small into the bar." They talk of the terrible things they have done and the wonderful things they will do. After he introduces them to Harvey, they leave feeling a little better. In this way, Elwood believes he helps the strangers he meets in profound ways.

The *Diagnostic and Statistical Manual, Fifth Edition* (DSM-5)[1] is a bedrock of psychology, but one of its flaws is

---

HARVEY

Directed by
Henry Koster

Cast
James Stewart as Elwood P. Dowd, Josephine Hull as Veta Louise Simmons, Peggy Dow as Miss Kelly, Charles Drake as Dr. Sanderson, Cecil Kellaway as Dr. Chumley

Oscar Wins
Best Actress in a Supporting Role (Jospehine Hull)

Oscar Nominations
Best Actor in a Leading Role (James Stewart)

Golden Globe Wins
Best Supporting Actress (Jospehine Hull)

Metascore: N/A

that it uses a medical model of pathology. In other words, it emphasizes the question, "What's wrong?" rather than asking, "What's right?" The field of psychology has had to fight hard to remember that health isn't just the absence of illness; likewise, the definition of impairment will vary depending on context. For Elwood and Lars, they both experienced an impaired sense of reality, yet they seemed to have an improved quality of life a result. Positive psychology is a movement that attempts to close this gap by proposing that the goal of therapists is "healing what is weak as well as nurturing what is strong".[2] This refreshing perspective on mental health is epitomized by the Lars' family physician who not only refuses to be alarmed about his delusion (since he is functioning and is not a harm to anyone), but leverages the delusion to help him come out of his shell. In the next chapter we bring Act I in for a landing with another double-feature that highlights the potential virtues of psychopathology, though with a more somber tone.

Notes

[1] American Psychiatric Association, (2013). *Diagnostic and statistical manual of mental disorders* (5th ed.). Washington, DC: Author.

[2] Seligman, M.E.P. (2002). Positive psychology, positive prevention, and positive therapy. In C.R. Snyder & S.J. Lopez (Eds.). *Handbook of Positive Psychology* (pp. 3-12). New York: Oxford.

Melancholia (2011) & Take Shelter (2011)

"Stay positive" maxims are deeply ingrained in American culture. But is the best course always to "look at the bright side," "pull up your bootstraps," "or "keep your nose to the grindstone?" The characters in this double-feature may not think so. They struggle with what might be called mental illness, but when put into the context of impending disaster, their illness looks less like delusion and more like clarity.

Degrees of Suffering

Melancholia begins with surrealistic and haunting imagery, then shifts in style and tone to a humorous, documentary-like scene of a bride and groom on their way to their wedding reception. More sharp contrasts follow, including the sisterly dynamic of the deeply depressed bride (Justine) and her seemingly got-it-together sister (Claire). It is revealed that a large planet is hurling towards earth on what might be a collision course. For most movies, this news would cause everyone to spring into action. But in this film the characters barely mention what might be coming, much less feel compelled to do anything about it. In the second half of the film, Justine's depression seems almost adaptive in her acceptance of disaster while Claire becomes increasingly unraveled as the cataclysmic moment approaches.

In *Take Shelter*, Curtis and Samantha are a mid-western husband and wife. Curtis is a good father who works a blue collar job and leads a happy life; however, he begins to have reoccurring nightmares of a terrorizing storm where the rain resembles oil and animals attack without reason. These dreams become so vivid that Curtis wonders if he is having a premonition or if he is exhibiting the same symptoms of schizophrenia this his mother had 30 years prior. He becomes obsessed with creating a tornado shelter where he will be able to protect his family. However his obsession comes at the cost of ostracizing him from his friends and, more importantly, his wife. *Take Shelter* goes beyond most psychological dramas in its ambition. Not only does it expand the spectrum between mental illness and a healthy, grounded perception, it tackles the profound subject of how family members support each other while one of its own becomes unhinged.

Functional Dysfunction

In terms of the DSM-5 criteria, both Justine and Curtis would meet criteria for Major Depressive Disorder and Schizophrenia, respectively. For a diagnosis of Major Depressive Disorder, 5 or more of the following symptoms over a two week period must be experienced[1]:

- Depressed mood most of the day, nearly every day
- Markedly diminished interest or pleasure in all, or almost all activities
- Significant weight loss or gain
- Insomnia or hypersomnia
- Psychomotor agitation or retardation
- Fatigue or loss of energy
- Feelings of worthlessness or excessive or inappropriate guilt
- Diminished ability to think or concentrating or indecisiveness
- Recurrent thoughts of death (not just fear of dying),

recurrent suicidal ideation

Clearly, Justine has a depressed mood, lack of interest in her own wedding and close friends, loss of energy, and diminished ability to communicate with others. She likely also has thoughts of death, sleeping issues, and feelings of worthlessness due to her acting out behavior.

The DSM-5 defines Schizophrenia as experiencing 2 or more of the following symptoms, each present for a significant portion of time during a 1-month period[2]:

- Delusions

- Hallucinations

- Disorganized speech (e.g., frequent derailment or incoherence)

- Grossly disorganized or catatonic behavior

- Negative symptoms (i.e., diminished emotional expression or avolition)

Curtis presents with fixed, false ideas (delusions), such as his belief that there will be a catastrophic storm and that their family dog will become aggressive and attack. He also shows signs of false perception (hallucinations) by way of phantom pain in his arm. The DSM-5 does caution against labeling a false perception as a hallucination if it is in the context of falling asleep (hypnagogic) or waking up (hypnopompic).[3] But

MELANCHOLIA

Directed by
Lars von Trier

Cast
Kirsten Dunst as Justine, Charlotte Gainsbourg as Claire, Alexander Skarsgard as Michael, Brady Corbet as Tim, Kiefer Sutherland as John

Metascore: 80

even with this caveat in mind, it seems that Curtis's sensations endure beyond these states.

Great films inspire us to feel what the character feels. What if all life on the planet was about to reach an abrupt end? Wouldn't most healthy people feel hopeless, depressed, or even frozen? Wouldn't any loving father and husband do everything in his power to protect his family from threats that seem imminent? If we can see through the lenses of each character's distorted sense of reality, their feelings and symptoms are expected, and even natural. In this way we can have great empathy for Justine and Curtis because all their dread and despair is felt for good reason. No matter how severe the reaction or illness, there is always at least one reason (even if the reason is not objectively true) for why people feel what they feel. If we assume that the events of *Melancholia* and *Take Shelter* are not perception and do in fact unfold, then "illness" is a type of clarity that the "healthy" do not possess. So who is to say what is healthy?

> **TAKE SHELTER**
>
> **Directed by**
> Jeff Nichols
>
> **Cast**
> Michael Shannon as Curtis, Jessica Chastain as Samantha, Tova Stewart as Hannah, Shea Whigham as Dewart, Katy Mixon as Nat, Natasha Randall as Cammie
>
> **Metascore: 85**

The term "pathology" comes from the Greek meaning "the study of suffering." Certainly, suffering afflicts more than those who are not delusional or depressed. As Psychiatrist M. Scott Peck states in the beginning of his landmark work, *The Road Less Traveled*, "life is difficult" and sometimes a healthy approach to life involves a great deal of suffering.[4] From this lens, Justine and Curtis may not be "healthy" as much as they are experiencing existential crises. The likelihood of everyone and everything they love being destroyed would cause any normal person to experience tremendous emotional turmoil. To claim that healthy people can't be anxious or depressed is to claim that healthy people never experience tragedy.

Before the field of western psychology was established by figures like Sigmund Feud and Carl Jung, philosophers and theologians were responsible for navigating the dense trail of human experience. Some of the most noteworthy forerunners were Soren Kierkegaard and Friedrich Nietzsche- 19th century existential philosophers. They certainly would have had a lot to say about Justine's and Curtis's predicament. In his book, *The Concept of Anxiety*, Kierkegaard remarks, "Anxiety is the dizziness of freedom."[5] For him, existence brings with it certain liabilities like anxiety and sorrow. We can't expect to travel through life unscathed (especially with extinction-level events and killer storms bearing down). We should keep this in mind as we transition to Act II on family dynamics, which can be rife with happiness and trauma in equal measure.

Notes

[1,2,3] American Psychiatric Association, (2013). *Diagnostic and statistical manual of mental disorders* (5th ed.). Washington, DC: Author.

[4] Peck, M. Scott. (2003) *The Road Less Traveled, Timeless Edition: A New Psychology of Love, Traditional Values and Spiritual Growth.* New York: Simon and Shuster.

[5] Kierkegaard, S. (2013) *Kierkegaard's Writings, VIII: Concept of Anxiety: A Simple Psychologically Orienting Deliberation on the Dogmatic Issue of Hereditary Sin: Concept of Anxiety v. 8*. Princeton: Princeton University.

CinemAnalysis

Act II

Family Thermo-Dynamics:

Parents, Children, and Siblings on Screen

Terms of Endearment (1983) & Postcards from the Edge (1990)

Family interactions have provided fodder for some of best material in film history. Movies about families resonate with audiences because we see ourselves (or our parents, or our siblings, or our children) in the characters. We've often lived through some version of what is on the screen (like a holiday dinner, a road trip, or sibling rivalry). Act II presents double features about brothers, sisters, fathers, and sons, and we start off with mothers and daughters.

Mommies Dearest

Terms of Endearment tells the story of Aurora and her daughter, Emma. The story spans decades, including Emma's coming of age, marriage, parenthood, divorce, and battle with cancer. Emma's relationship with her mother is certainly strained at times, in large part because Aurora is a piece of work. Aurora has a number of devoted suitors, but the guy who finally cracks her icy exterior is next door neighbor Garrett, an ex-astronaut. After one of the worst first dates ever captured on film, the two form a bond that in turn helps Aurora connect with Emma.

Postcards from the Edge wasn't nearly as acclaimed as *Terms of Endearment*, but is very entertaining in its own right. It was written by Carrie Fisher and is based on her relationship with her mother, Debbie Reynolds. Suzanne is an actress getting out of rehab and struggling to emerge from the shadow of her famous mother, Doris, (Shirley MacLaine, who also played Aurora in *Terms of Endearment*). The tone shifts back and forth between hilarious (such as Suzanne filming a hanging rooftop scene for a cop movie) and serious (any number of confrontations between narcissistic Doris and drug-addicted Suzanne). *Postcards from the Edge* isn't close to the tearjerker that *Terms of Endearment* is, but it still tugs at the heartstrings.

These maternal movies are about more than the love-hate nature of many mother-daughter relationships. A shared theme is the importance of accepting those you love for who they are- appreciating their gifts and letting go their foibles. In each, it's more the daughter who has to let things go (and both Aurora and Doris have plenty for their daughters to deal with). But the daughters have their share of issues, too (divorce, drug addiction, career troubles).

It's Like When You Say One Thing but Bean Your Mother . . .

To varying degrees both Suzanne and Emma suffer from the failure to launch phenomenon. Suzanne is a total mess with her drug addiction and career in shambles. There are several moments in *Postcards from the Edge* when she comes off like a stunted adolescent. Emma is further along the maturity continu-

---

TERMS OF ENDEARMENT

Directed by
James L. Brooks

Cast
Shirley MacLaine as Aurora Greenway, Debra Winger as Emma Horton, Jack Nicholson as Garrett Breedlove, Danny DeVito as Vernon Dahlart, Jeff Daniels as Flap Horton

Oscar Wins
Best Picture
Best Director
Best Writing, Screenplay Based on Material from Another Medium
Best Actress in a Leading Role (Shirley MacLaine)
Best Actor in a Supporting Role (Jack Nicholson)

Oscar Nominations
Best Actress in a Leading Role (Debra Winger)
Best Actor in a Supporting Role (John Lithgow)
Bes Music, Original Score
Best Film Editing
Best Art Direction-Set Decoration
Best Sound

Golden Globe Wins
Best Motion Picture – Drama
Best Director – Motion Picture
Best Performance by an Actress in a Motion Picture (Shirley MacLaine)
Best Performance by an Actor in a Supporting Role in a Motion Picture (Jack Nicholson)
Screenplay – Motion Picture

Metascore: 79

um, but her marriage and motherhood are held together (if at all) by spit and bailing wire. Both Emma and Suzanne have interactions with their mothers that smack of adolescence. Research has shown a link between an adult child's failure to attain expected adult status (like family and career), the mother's state of mind, and the degree of ambivalence in the relationship.[1] The mothers' states of mind in these films share striking similarities in terms of protectiveness mixed with envy about what opportunities await their daughters. When daughters are children it is pretty obvious to all involved that their needs are paramount. But when both daughters and mothers are adults, it is less clear whose needs take precedence. Earlier patterns of interaction with mothers as advice-givers become obsolete as daughters acquire skills that may surpass those of their mothers (especially when daughters become mothers themselves). Later in life, mothers come to view their offspring as the legacy that will outlive them.[2] At the end of *Postcards from the Edge* Doris as much as acknowledges to Suzanne that she is her legacy; Doris laments that her "turn" is over and that Suzanne needs to cherish her turn.

> **POSTCARDS FROM THE EDGE**
>
> **Directed by**
> Mike Nichols
>
> **Cast**
> Meryl Streep as Suzanne Vale, Shirley MacLaine as Doris Mann, Dennis Quaid as Jack Faulkner, Gene Hackman as Lowell Kolchek, Richard Dreyfuss as Dr. Frankenthal, Rob Reiner as Joe Pierce
>
> **Oscar Nominations**
> Best Actress in a Leading Role (Shirley MacLaine)
> Best Music, Original Song "I'm Checkin' Out"
>
> **Metascore: 71**

Ambivalence as a psychological term captures the idea of the love-hate relationship. It is the coexistence within an individual of positive and negative feelings toward the same person, simultaneously drawing her or him in opposite directions. Ambivalence is interactional—individuals evaluate social relations (like that between a mother and adult daughter) as simultaneously positive and negative. As it turns out, ambivalence increases under conditions of potential dependence, as opposed to the support that is regularly given to family members.[3] So it makes sense that the ambivalence would be ratcheted up for Suzanne and Doris, since Suzanne is legally bound to live with Doris as a condition of her release from rehab. Emma also has to lean hard on Aurora given her various life struggles. In addition, research has shown that certain factors contribute to ambivalence in parent-adult child relationships, including dyads of women (check for Aurora/Emma and Doris/Suzanne), among those in poor health (check for both, including Suzanne's addiction), and for adult children with poor parental relations early in life (we can only imagine).[4] Given all of these risk factors, it's a wonder these daughters and mothers manage to get along at all. But there's enough love there to pull back the love-hate pendulum a bit closer to the middle.

Notes

[1] Pillemer, K., & Suitor, J.J. (2002). Explaining mothers' ambivalence toward their adult children. *Journal of Marriage and Family, 64*, 602-613.

[2] Fingerman, K.L. (2001). *Aging Mothers and Their Adult Daughters: A Study in Mixed Emotions*. New York: Springer.

[3] Willson, A.E., Shuey, K.M., Elder Jr., G.H., & Wickrama, K.A.S. (2006). Ambivalence in mother-adult child relations: A dyadic analysis. *Social Psychology Quarterly, 69*, 235-252.

[4] Willson, A.E., Shuey, K.M., & Elder Jr., G.H. (2002). Ambivalence in the relationship of adult children to aging parents and in-laws. *Journal of Marriage and Family, 65*, 1055-1072.

Nothing in Common (1986) & Big Fish (2003)

Having looked at mother-daughter relationships, we now turn to a pair of films about the bonds between fathers and their adult sons. It's too simplistic to clump issues by gender (like "mother-daughter friction" or "father-son rivalry") because the same psychological problems can plague both women and men. That being said, sons should be forewarned- these next two movies may strike a nerve, but both deliver gratifying pay-offs and some laughs along the way.

Story Arc of the Patriarch

Nothing in Common is about the exploits of hot-shot advertising executive David Basner, as well as his father, Max, and mother, Lorraine. Early in the story David is so busy with his career and being a player that he's ambushed when Lorraine leaves Max, who turns out was also a hot-shot and a player (even as a married man) back in his day. David and Max don't have much use for each other, but when Max is diagnosed with diabetes, David has to step up with Lorraine out of the picture. The son then has to assume the parent role, including making some career sacrifices to care for his ailing father. The heavy themes are balanced by some really funny material (the scene when Basner loses it during a commercial shoot is a riot).

Big Fish is a rare foray into drama for director Tim Burton. But Burton being Burton, *Big Fish* has plenty of

> **Nothing in Common**
>
> **Directed by**
> Gary Marshall
>
> **Cast**
> Tom Hanks as David Basner, Jackie Gleason as Max Basner, Eva Marie Saint as Lorraine Basner, Hector Elizondo as Charlie Gargas, Barry Corbin as Andrew Woolridge
>
> **Metascore:** 62

quirky visual touches that serve the story-telling nicely. Will Bloom is struggling to emerge from the shadow of his father, Ed, a man who never met a big tale he didn't like to tell. Unlike *Nothing in Common*, *Big Fish* takes the audience back in time to meet the youthful Ed and the love of his life, Sandra. By the end of the movie Will learns to stop resenting his father and comes to understand how Ed transformed his life memories into whimsical yarns. In essence, Ed created a family folklore, and Will ultimately cherishes it. *Big Fish* is at once a typical Tim Burton movie and a movie unlike any of his others.

> **BIG FISH**
>
> **Directed by**
> Tim Burton
>
> **Cast**
> Ewan McGregor as Ed Bloom (Young), Albert Finney as Ed Bloom (Senior), Billy Crudup as Will Bloom, Jessica Lange as Sandra Bloom (Senior), Helena Bonham Carter as Jenny, Marion Cotillard as Josephine Bloom
>
> **Oscar Nominations**
> Best Music, Original Score
>
> **Metascore: 58**

Daddy Issues

Conventional wisdom holds that the mother-child bond is crucial for healthy development. But research suggests that the effect of father love on offspring's development is as powerful as the effect of mother love, and sometimes even more so. In fact, father love appears to be as heavily implicated as mother love in offsprings' psychological well-being and health, as well as in an array of psychological and behavioral problems.[1] So the fact that David and Will were so significantly affected by their relationships with Max and Ed, respectively, is not surprising.

The National Child Development Study explored parent-child relationships and showed that a stronger bond between a son and father was associated with a stronger bond between son and *mother*, as well as early father involvement and fewer emotional and behavioral problems in adolescence.[2] In *Nothing in Common*, David and Lorraine are also a bit estranged, and it's pretty obvious that their detachment is collateral damage from the David-Max impasse. A big issue between Will and Ed in *Big Fish* is trust (Will doesn't believe in the veracity of Ed's various yarns). Ed and Sandra are together, but parental divorce can erode trust according to findings from the Marital Instability over the Life Course Study; although parental divorce was negatively associated with trust, those effects largely disappeared once the quality of the past parent-teen relationship is taken into account. The one exception is trust in fathers where children of divorce remain at higher risk of mistrust (see David and Max). Trust (in parents, intimates, and others) is strongly linked to positive parent-teen relationships regardless of parental divorce.[3] So even children of married parents, like Will, can have long-standing problems rooted in strained father-son connections during adolescence.

    The divorce of Max and Lorraine drops like a bomb on David's gilded life. The Binuclear Family Study explored children's perceptions of their parents' divorce and its long-term effects. Although most adult children felt that their relationships with their fathers had either improved or remained stable over time, increased inter-parental conflict (like Max and Lorraine clashing), early father remarriage, and low father involvement in the early post-divorce years were associated with worsening relationships. Custody did not directly affect relationship quality between fathers and sons[4], so physical proximity is not the factor that it would seem to be. The other bomb for David is Max's diabetes. But ultimately, caring for his father is what pushes the two of them together. Two major risk factors were removed from their relationship: inter-parental conflict (with his parents living apart, they can't fight) and low involvement post-divorce. For struggling adult sons and fathers, the recipe for reconciliation would probably be some shared or collaborative endeavor (ideally not involving a life-threatening medical condition).

Notes

[1] Rohner, R.P., & Veneziano, R.A. (2001). The importance of father love: History and contemporary evidence. *Review of General Psychology*, *5*, 382-405.

[2] Flouri, E., & Buchanan, A. (2002). What predicts good relationships with parents in adolescence and partners in adult life: Findings from the 1958 British birth cohort. *Journal of Family Psychology*, *16*, 186-198.

[3] King, V. (2002). Parental divorce and interpersonal trust in adult offspring. *Journal of Marriage and Family*, *64*, 642-656.

[4] Ahrons, C.R., & Tanner, J.L. (2003). Adult Children and Their Fathers: Relationship Changes 20 Years After Parental Divorce. *Family Relations*, *52*, 340-351.

The Royal Tenenbaums (2001) & Little Miss Sunshine (2006)

Now we widen the lens to consider parents' relationships with multiple children, and siblings' relationships with each other. This double feature includes numerous wacky characters, frayed bonds, and crazy moments. So basically they're about normal families.

You Can't Pick Your Family

The Royal Tenenbaums is about the eponymous family, led (sort of) by patriarch and rascal Royal. Royal is estranged from his wife and his three adult children- Chas, Margot (who was adopted), and Richie. These people have more issues than the New York Times. Chas (having lost his wife) is neurotically overprotective of his two sons, Margot is in an unhealthy and secretive marriage, and Richie is deeply in love with Margot (remember, she's adopted). Also in orbit is Eli, a childhood friend of the Tenenbaum kids who wants to be part of the gang. The good news is that everyone makes some inroads towards mental health, but not before a few emotional meltdowns.

Little Miss Sunshine tells of the Hoover family's road trip to get young Olive to the Little Miss Sunshine beauty pageant for girls in California. Olive is by far the most grounded and stable member of her blended family- her dad, Richard, is a down-on-his-luck aspiring self-help guru, Uncle Frank is suicidal, step-brother Dwayne has taken a vow of silence, her grandfather is a drug addict, and her mom is on the edge of breakdown trying to hold everybody together. At the start of the trip everyone is at each other's throats (and much of the verbal sparring is hilarious), but they slowly pull together as they near the pageant. A recurring sight gag becomes a nice metaphor- the family has to push start their Volkswagen van every time they hit the road. Blood is definitely thicker than water when the grown-ups come to Olive's aid at the pageant (one of the greatest musical finales in movie history).

The grandfathers in both of these movies first come across as real jerks. But their rough exteriors slowly melt away, thanks largely to their connections with their grandchildren. Each guy meets his end by film's end, but they first manage to connect with their own children. There's a touching scene in *Tenebaums* when Chas admits to Royal that he needs help to overcome his phobia of losing his children. And the spirit of Grandpa Hoover is alive and well when Olive takes to the stage at the pageant.

> **THE ROYAL TENENBAUMS**
>
> **Directed by**
> Wes Anderson
>
> **Cast**
> Gene Hackman as Royal Tenenbaum, Anjelica Huston as Etheline Tenenbaum, Ben Stiller as Chas Tenenbaum, Gwyneth Paltrow as Margot Tenenbaum, Luke Wilson as Richi Tenenbaum, Owen Wilson as Eli Cash, Bill Murray as Raleigh St. Clair, Alec Baldwin as Narrator
>
> **Oscar Nominations**
> Best Writing, Screenplay Written Directly for the Screen
>
> **Golden Globe Wins**
> Best Performance by an Actor in a Motion Picture – Comedy or Musical (Gene Hackman)
>
> **Metascore: 75**

Family Systems

Murray Bowen is best known for his writing on family systems theory and how a person works to differentiate self from others. He believes that a healthy family is composed of individuals who cultivate harmony between two competing drives: individuality and connectedness.[1] An unhealthy family is one that strives too fervently for conformity at the expense of individuality, or individuality at the expense of connection.[2] So the key is balance. For the Hoovers of *Little Miss Sunshine*, Richard pushes his kids towards conformity with his heavy-handed dispensing of advice, while Dwayne's vow of silence fights with equal force to be an island, cut off from others. By the way, Dwayne's vow is an effort to improve self-discipline in preparation for a career in the Air Force; so he wants to sequester himself in the short-term with the goal of long-term disengagement. For the Tenenbaums, early on the family strongly praised (perhaps too strongly) the children's individuality more so than their connectedness; as a result, Margot is much like Dwayne in the way she locks herself in the bathroom for hours on end. Chas wants nothing to do with his father and only cares about being connected with his boys. Poor Eli seems to be craving the approval of the family in the hopes of being an honorary member (he even goes so far as to have an affair with Margot when they grow up).

> **LITTLE MISS SUNSHINE**
>
> **Directed by**
> Jonathan Dayton & Valerie Faris
>
> **Cast**
> Abigail Breslin as Olive Hoover, Greg Kinnear as Richard Hoover, Toni Collette as Sheryl Hoover, Paul Dano Dwayne, Alan Arkin Grandpa Edwin Hoover, Steve Carrell as Frank Ginsberg, Bryan Cranston as Stan Grossman, Dean Norris as State Trooper McCleary
>
> **Oscar Wins**
> Best Performance by an Actor in a Supporting Role (Alan Arkin)
> Best Writing, Original Screenplay
>
> **Oscar Nominations**
> Best Motion Picture of the Year
> Best Performance by an Actress in a Supporting Role (Abigail Breslin)
>
> **Metascore: 80**

The drama of the Tenenbaums and the Hoovers centers around how each character strives for more connectedness or individuation, sometimes for their good and sometimes to their detriment. Royal might be the first of his family to attempt to correct his mistakes of selfish individuality and instead become more connected. At first, Chas believes it's too little, too late, and feels more compelled to be ultra-controlling of his sons' safety; but later, he softens and reaches out to his dad while letting go of some control of his sons. For the Hoovers, Frank follows a similar arc. He individuates by moving past his romantic rejection and connects with the rest of the Hoover family. Dwayne reaches out and, in a sense, conforms to the family (in a healthy way), while Richard gives Olive the freedom to perform her eccentric dance on stage. Olive almost succumbs to the pressures of beauty pageant conformity but the family provides her with much needed connectedness when they back her up during her musical number, which actually enables her to be herself.

The movement towards improved relationships is the reason why both stories are so heartwarming. This improved relational health is attributable to corrective changes that each individual character makes. The characters work out various challenges related to Bowens' concept of differentiation. One outcome is closer relationships between siblings, which is where we head next.

Notes

[1] Gilbert, Roberta. (2004). *The eight concepts of Bowen Theory*. Falls Church, VA: Leading Systems Press.

[2] Kerr, M.E. (2003). *One family's story: A primer on Bowen Theory*. Washington D.C.: Bowen Center for the Study of the Family.

The Fabulous Baker Boys (1989) & Big Night (1996)

These movies are linked by their exploration of brotherhood and the emotive power of music and food, respectively. Whereas the previous double feature involved parents and children, these films focus on pairs of siblings. In fact, parents are entirely absent from the stories.

It's a Bro Thing

The Fabulous Baker Boys are Jack and Frank, played by real-life brothers Jeff and Beau Bridges, a couple of pianists who had been earning a decent living for years playing gigs in the Seattle area. But struggling to survive in a changing nightlife environment, they break with their tandem-piano routine and bring on Susie Diamond, a down-on-her-luck singer.

> **THE FABULOUS BAKER BOYS**
>
> **Directed by**
> Steve Kloves
>
> **Cast**
> Jeff Bridges as Jack Baker, Michelle Pfeiffer as Susie Diamond, Beau Bridges as Frank Baker, Ellie Raab as Nina
>
> **Oscar Nominations**
> Best Actress in a Leading Role (Michelle Pfeiffer)
> Best Cinematography
> Best Film Editing
> Best Music, Original Score
>
> **Golden Globe Wins**
> Best Performance by an Actress in a Motion Picture – Drama (Michelle Pfeiffer)
> Best Original Score – Motion Picture
>
> **Metascore:** N/A

The brothers in *Big Night* are Italian immigrant restaurateurs Primo and Secundo (talk about functional names). Primo is a brilliant chef who steadfastly resists Americanizing their family recipes. Secundo is the more practical, business-minded of the two. The story is driven by Primo and Secundo's preparation for a "big night" dinner which they hope a celebrity will attend to give their restaurant much-needed publicity.

> **BIG NIGHT**
>
> **Directed by**
> Campbell Scott & Stanley Tucci
>
> **Cast**
> Marc Anthony as Cristiano, Tony Shalhoub as Primo, Stanley Tucci as Secondo, Minnie Driver as Phyllis, Liev Schreiber as Leo, Allison Janney as Ann, Ian Holm as Pascal
>
> **Metascore: 80**

The younger brothers in each of these films are rakes. Jack's predilection for seduction gets him involved with Susie (but he can hardly be blamed after her smoldering rendition of "Makin' Whoopee" atop a grand piano). Their affair ostensibly leads to the break-up of the Baker act. But the real reason is that Jack, actually a talented jazz musician, has to break free of the cocktail grind. Secundo doesn't have his brother's cooking talent (he's more like Frank in that regard), and his self-destructive libido contributes to some very hard luck for their beleaguered restaurant.

The two strained fraternal relationships are pushed to the breaking point, but they bounce back. Naturally, the Bakers reconcile while tickling the ivories, while Primo and Secundo's rapprochement takes place in the kitchen.

Birth Order and Personality

The narratives in this double feature are largely driven by the clichéd sibling dynamic of the straight-laced, high-achieving older brother and the rebellious younger brother. But is there anything to these stereotypes? Several studies suggest yes. One study looked at birth order effects on personality in a series of studies that included over 1,000 families. Looking at several personality dimensions, first-borns were nominated as most achieving and most conscientious (ala *Baker Boys'* Frank and *Big Night's* Primo). In contrast, later-borns were nominated as most rebellious, liberal, and agreeable (ala Jack and Secundo). The same results were obtained whether or not birth order was made salient to the raters (which would activate stereotypes) during the personality ratings.[1] Another study found that firstborns were more achieving and conscientious than secondborns and that secondborns were more rebellious and open to new experiences than firstborns.[2] These and other studies support the niche model of personality development: personalities of siblings vary because they adopt different strategies for gaining parental favor. For example, eldest children identify with parents and authority, supporting the status quo, while younger children rebel against the status quo.[3] Prequels to *The Fabulous Baker Boys* and *Big Night* could provide interesting back stories about how the brothers came to be who they are. What were there personalities like as children? Adolescents? What role did their parents play in reinforcing the achievement orientations of Frank and Primo, and the rebelliousness of Jack and Secundo? Until such projects get the green light, we'll be left to wonder, but it's not a stretch to assume that these guys had similar personalities and relationships as youngsters.

Notes

[1] Paulhus, D.L., Trapnell, P.D., and Chen, D. (1999). Birth order effects on personality and achievement within families. *Psychological Science, 10*, 482-488.

[2] Healey, M.D., & Ellis, B.J. (2007). Birth order, conscientiousness, and openness to experience: Tests of the family-niche model of personality using a within-family methodology. *Evolution and Human Behavior, 28*, 55-59.

[3] Sulloway, F.J. (1996). *Born to Rebel: Birth Order, Family Dynamics and Creative Lies.* New York: Pantheon.

You Can Count on Me (2000) & The Darjeeling Limited (2007)

These two movies center on adult sibling relationships (sister-brother and trio of brothers). In each, the siblings reunite sometime after the death of parents. How the individuals respond to their parents' death certainly is a factor, but not the whole story.

Birds of a Feather

In *You Can Count on Me*, Sammie reunites with her brother, Terry. Their first lunch together is a great depiction of bottled up emotion. Sammie and Terry have sharp differences about how to live and what the tragic death of their parents has taught them about the world. Sammie is the responsible one who works at a bank, goes to church, and thoughtfully raises her 9 year-old son Rudy, who incidentally is just about the same age they were when their parents died is a car crash. Terry is a drifter, moving wherever the wind blows him. He sadly, yet honestly, believes that no one has any real purpose, life has no big meaning, and their parents' death was not part of a plan. Their differences almost drive them apart before they can really go back to the relationship, back to their connection and dependence to each other that the name of the movie implies.

The Darjeeling Limited depicts

> **YOU CAN COUNT ON ME**
>
> **Directed by**
> Kenneth Lonergan
>
> **Cast**
> Laura Linney as Samantha Prescott, Mark Ruffalo as Terry Prescott, Matthew Broderick as Brian Everett, Rory Culkin as Rudy Prescott, Jon Tenney as Bob Steegerson
>
> **Oscar Nominations**
> Best Actress in a Leading Role (Laura Linney)
> Best Writing, Screenplay Written Directly for the Screen
>
> **Metascore: 85**

quirkier, but equally profound family differences, alliances, and dysfunction. The story picks up long after the death of a father, after which his 3 sons dispersed in shock and then led lives apart from each other. The brothers- Peter, Francis, and Jack- reunite on a train trip (on the Darjeeling Limited) through India. Francis summarizes their mission: "Be completely open and say yes to everything even if it's shocking and painful." Plenty of shock and pain follows, but some laughs soften the blows. Their mother lives in India and has checked out emotionally due to her continued grief. Her sons fail to reconnect with her on the trip, but they manage to reconnect with each other.

Both of these films open in disorienting fashion. In the first scene of *You Can Count on Me*, a husband and wife are driving on a back road at night. They only have a moment of screen time, yet their brief dialogue enables the audience to begin connecting with them. Then ... *crash*. They are gone- torn from the movie just as they are from the lives of their orphaned children. *The Darjeeling Limited* also throws the audience an early curve ball. The first several moments feature a character played by Bill Murray (a regular in director Wes Anderson's films), giving the impression that he will figure prominently in the story. He is racing to make the train as it is pulling out of the station. Instead, Adrien Brody's character passes him and hops the train. It's a post-modern, passing-of-the-torch moment from Murray to Brody, who is young enough to play the part of a brother and run fast enough to make the train.

Sibling Attachment

John Bowlby first published his theory of attachment in 1988. Since then, his theories continue to be widely researched and used in clinical practice, particularly concerning infants bonding with parents in the first years of life. More recently, attachment theory has been applied to adult bonding with couples, siblings and other intimate relationships.[1] These two films give a rich picture of sibling attachment in later stages of the life cycle.

The bond between *You Can Count on Me's* Sammie and Terry does not reveal itself because they are cut from the same cloth. In fact, the opposite is true - their bond comes from their unwavering commitment to each other despite their differences. The title speaks directly to this point (which, incidentally, is not uttered at any point in the movie).

Peter, Francis, and Jack from *The Darjeeling Limited* are on a journey to reconnect and "become brothers again." In both films, but especially *The Darjeeling Limited*, the pursuit to reconnect sibling attachment is largely due to the unwanted "detachment" of a lost parent. Francis somehow knows that the loss of their father leads them to a greater need to be connected with each other. His brothers and mother also show signs that they desire this reconnection and yet they are somewhat paralyzed by their loss (their mother especially so). In the end both sets of siblings are shown in a process of reattaching. They don't quite get all the way there, but not everybody does.

THE DARJEELING LIMITED

Directed by
Wes Anderson

Cast
Owen Wilson as Francis, Adrien Brody as Peter, Jason Schwartzman as Jack, Amara Karan as Rita, Irrfan Khan as The Father, Bill Murray as The Businessman, Anjelica Huston as Patricia

Metascore: 67

Act II has been about families. More specifically, we have looked at how family members relate to one another. In the next Act we look at the individual and various forms of identity, including how identities form and change.

Notes

[1] Reed, M.D. (1993). Sudden death and bereavement outcomes: The impact of resources on grief symptomatology and detachment. *Suicide and Life-Threatening Behavior, 23*, 204–220.

Act III

Through the Looking Glass:

Identity on Film

Up in the Air (2009) & The Accidental Tourist (1988)

What is identity? The obvious answer is- *who we are*. Peeling back the onion, it's how we view ourselves and how others view us. It's how we relate to others and, in turn, how others relate to us. Identity can unfold over time, contingent on life stage and circumstances. To get things rolling about identify, here is a double-feature about men who choose to put various walls around themselves emotionally, and how they come to dismantle those walls.

On the Road Again (and again, and again, and . . .)

Up in the Air is the story of Ryan, who lives out of his suitcase flying around the country as a professional "down-sizer" (he's hired by companies to fire their employees). He's a loner who seems to savor lowering the boom on careers and livelihoods. He loves his business-class lifestyle (he gives lectures on how to live with a "light backpack") and abhors being grounded, even briefly, at his firm's Omaha headquarters. He's also fiercely determined to amass as many frequent flyer miles as possible- a strange quest, but it leads to an unexpected act of selflessness (once he's come around to the fact that it's not all about him).

Two events rock Ryan's intrepid/insular existence. First, he meets (in an airport, naturally) and then falls for Alex, another white collar mercenary who turns out to be a little too much like Ryan for his own good. Second, he is forced to mentor a younger colleague, Natalie, who has designs of reinventing the whole downsizing-for-hire industry with video conferencing (if getting fired is unpleasant, how about being shown the door via computer monitor?). Despite his initial resentment of Natalie, Ryan comes to respect and support her.

The Accidental Tourist is the story of Macon, a business traveler of a much different sort. Arguably more introverted than Ryan, Macon loathes traveling and has become an expert on how to make it as pleasant as possible. His tips (such as always bring a book on a plane so that other passengers won't bother you) are collected in a series of books he has written as "The Accidental Tourist."

Macon's world is turned upside down by the murder of his 12 year-old son and consequent estrangement from his wife, Sarah. And if all that weren't enough, Macon becomes incapacitated due to a fall down some stairs and has to stay with his eccentric siblings. He hires Muriel to train the unruly dog who belonged to his son. Muriel's quirkiness is in stark contrast to Macon's introversion, but the two develop a romance that brings him out of his shell.

Both Ryan and Macon become more connected to others. Along the way Ryan reconciles (at least a little bit) with his two sisters. Macon steps into the next chapter of his life. Neither go through a complete transformation- and that narrative restraint makes their stories more believable and powerful.

UP IN THE AIR

Directed by
Jason Reitman

Cast
George Clooney as Ryan Bingham, Vera Farmiga as Alex Goran, Anna Kendrick as Natalie Keener, Jason Bateman as Craig Gregory, Amy Morton as Kara Bingham, J.K. Simmons as Bob, Danny McBride as Jim Miller, Zach Galifianakis as Steve

Oscar Nominations
Best Motion Picture of the Year
Best Achievement in Directing
Best Performance by an Actor in a Leading Role (George Clooney)
Best Performance by an Actress in a Supporting Role (Anna Kendrick)
Best Performance by an Actress in a Supporting Role (Vera Farmiga)
Best Writing, Adapted Screenplay

Golden Globe Wins
Best Screenplay - Motion Picture

Metascore: 83

Fear of Intimacy

Ryan and Macon both display a fear of intimacy- and not just of the romantic sort. A big reason Ryan likes being on the road so much is that he can be independent. For him, happiness is traveling with a "light backpack." In contrast, Macon steers clear of relationships by wanting to stay close to home, or bringing home with him when he travels (his brand is represented as a living room chair with wings). Fear of intimacy is a psychological construct that has been researched a great deal. One way it has been examined is through adult attachment, such as sibling to sibling (see *You Can Count on Me* and *The Darjeeling Limited*). Many theorists conceptualize fear of intimacy as being multidimensional with components such as love and affection, personal validation, trust, and self-disclosure. One study had 360 college students complete a questionnaire about intimacy and the results supported the existence of these components, and also found that women and men differed in their experiences of intimacy.[1] Ryan is contrasted with both Alex and Natalie along these lines. Both of these women are achievement-oriented, career-first professionals like Ryan. When Ryan gets too intimate to Alex, though, it backfires. But his deepening platonic connection to Natalie pays off, big time.

> **THE ACCIDENTAL TOURIST**
>
> **Directed by**
> Lawrence Kasdan
>
> **Cast**
> William Hurt as Macon Leary, Kathleen Turner as Sarah Leary, Geena Davis as Muriel Pritchett, Amy Wright as Rose Leary, David Ogden Stiers as Porter Leary, Ed Begley Jr. as Charles Leary, Bill Pullman as Julian
>
> **Oscar Wins**
> Best Actress in a Supporting Role (Geena Davis)
>
> **Oscar Nominations**
> Best Picture
> Best Music, Original Score
> Best Writing, Screenplay Based on Material from Another Medium
>
> **Metascore: 53**

Macon showed signs of perfectionism (maybe even obsessive-compulsive disorder, when you see him with his cabinet-organizing siblings). Research has shown that perfectionism interferes with close, interpersonal relationships. For instance, maladaptive perfectionists (like alphabetizers of canned goods) reported significantly greater fear of intimacy than non-perfectionists.[2] Research has also shown a link between shame and intimacy fears, as well as self-blaming. Shame-prone individuals may be more likely to engage in self-deprecating thoughts and blame themselves for issues, perhaps making intimacy something to fear.[3] Macon likely feels a fair amount of shame wrapped up in the disclosure of feelings, of the untidiness of emotionality. As Ryan moves along in his story, he shows slivers of shame related to his estranged relationship with his family (and maybe his ruthless line of work?). In any event, Macon and Ryan both make strides in overcoming their intimacy fears, even though only one of them gets the girl.

Notes

[1] Hook, M.K., Gerstein, L.H., Detterich, L., & Gridley, B. (2003). How close are we? Measuring intimacy and examining gender differences. *Journal of Counseling and Development, 81,* 462-472.

[2] Martin, J.L., & Ashby, J.S. (2004). Perfectionism and fear of intimacy: Implications for relationships. *The Family Journal, 12,* 368-374.

[3] Lutwak, N., Panish, J., & Ferrari, J. (2003). Shame and guilt: Characterological vs. behavioral self-blame and their relationship to fear of intimacy. *Personality and Individual Differences, 35,* 909-916.

Sideways (2004) & Bunny and the Bull (2009)

Bromance- that glorious portmanteau of "brother" and "romance." This double-feature of "bromantic comedies" captures not only the mayhem of male bonding, but also the mystery (ever wonder about the guys with divergent personalities who have somehow become buddies?). These movies serve up both outrageous and touching moments about the loyalty of close friendships. And for better or for worse, a big part of a man's identity is defined by the friends he keeps.

I Love You, Man!

The middle-aged buddies of *Sideways* are Miles and Jack, who were college friends. Jack is about to be married and Best Man Miles drives him to Napa Valley to celebrate his last days as a bachelor. Miles is a wine sophisticate and a depressed (and probably alcoholic) one at that. Jack is a television and commercial actor who wants to party. He's a Peter Pan, essentially, and early on he states his intention to loosen up Miles (get him laid, actually). That's a tall order, given that Miles is a real piece of work; he's struggling to get past his divorce, unsuccessful writing career, and general lack of direction. Undaunted, Jack goes into full-throttle womanizing mode and jeopardizes his engagement. Fortunately for Miles, he starts up a romance with Maya, a fellow oenophile who seems far more capable of helping him out of his life funk than his college roommate.

Bunny and the Bull is a quirky British comedy about Steven (who has a fear of crowds and public places), who relives a road trip through Europe he had with his best friend, Bunny. Steven's apartment surrealistically transforms into the scenes of his memories, ala the imaginative visuals of films like *The Science of Sleep* (2006). The archetypes of the sensible-yet-uptight and the reckless-yet-lovable are embodied in Steven and Bunny just as they are for Miles and Jack, respectively. *Bunny and the Bull* depicts some of the same kinds of boys-will-be-boys antics as *Sideways*, though with less emotional depth.

The Balance Needed to Bounce Back

As we've already mentioned, positive psychology emphasizes what is right with a person, as opposed to searching for problems to fix. This often involves identifying and then nurturing characteristics that enable one to cope with life's challenges. Resiliency theory is defined as an individual's ability to bounce back when facing adversity.[1] One appealing aspect of resiliency theory is how it describes the thriving individual, not just the suffering person (or the person with psychopathology). Research on resiliency has identified three core personality types: resilient, over-controlled, and under-controlled.[2] Miles and Steven represent the over-controlled type. Steven is so controlled that venturing out into the world provokes bouts of anxiety. Miles may seem like a mere wine snob ("If they order Merlot, I'm leaving!"), but he is wound tight as a drum. Jack and Bunny are of the under-controlled

> **SIDEWAYS**
>
> **Directed by**
> Alexander Payne
>
> **Cast**
> Paul Giamatti as Miles, Thomas Haden Church as Jack, Virginia Madsen as Maya, Sandra Oh as Stephanie
>
> **Oscar Wins**
> Best Writing, Adapted Screenplay
>
> **Oscar Nominations**
> Best Motion Picture of the Year
> Best Achievement in Directing
> Best Performance by an Actor in a Supporting Role (Thomas Haden Church)
> Best Performance by an Actress in a Supporting Role (Virginia Madsen)
>
> **Golden Globe Wins**
> Best Motion Picture – Comedy or Musical
> Best Screenplay – Motion Picture
>
> **Metascore: 94**

type. Their impulses are not regulated by consequences or long term gratification. Jack could quite easily lose the marriage he is about to enter and Bunny throws caution to the wind when he wants the thrill of fighting a raging bull.

> **BUNNY AND THE BULL**
>
> **Directed by**
> Paul King
>
> **Cast**
> Edward Hogg as Stephen, Simon Farnaby as Bunny, Veronica Echegui as Eloisa, Julian Barratt as Atilla
>
> **Metascore: N/A**

So how could guys with such disparate personality types (over- and under-controlled) become friends? How do such bromances get so entrenched? In short, each member of the tandem needs some of what the other has. Steven and Miles need to let go of some of their control, while Bunny and Jack need to exercise more of it. Unfortunately, what generally plays out in both films is not poignant personal growth, but rather a great deal of parallel dysfunction (sadness is the prevailing emotion as each story winds down). Bunny and Jack don't budge much, if at all, in the direction of a resilient personality type. But there are sparks of hope for Steven and Miles. Maybe a bit of their friends rubbed off on them, because they show signs of letting go. For Miles this involves getting past his ex-wife with a cherished bottle of wine. And Steven can dare to face the wider world. If they keep moving in that direction they may yet become resilient individuals with much healthier identities.

Notes

[1] Bernard, B. (1991). *Fostering Resiliency in Kids: Protective Factors in the Family, School and Community.* Retrieved from http://www.wested.org/cs/we/view/rs/93.

[2] Hoermann, S., Zupanick, C.E. & Dambeck, M. (2011) *Interperson-*

al Difficulties in Specific Personality Disorders. Retrieved from http://www.mentalhelp.net/poc/view_doc.php?type=doc&id=476&cn=8.

October Sky (1999) & Searching for Bobby Fischer (1993)

A great deal of identify formation takes place during childhood. That forming comes from a person's innate characteristics (often referred to as "nature"), as well as from environmental factors (or "nurture"). This double-feature pairs two true stories about boys forging identities through an interplay of nature and nurture factors. They each discover incredible talents within themselves and then develop those talents with the support of mentors who bolster their resiliency.

Sometimes It Is Rocket Science

October Sky tells the story of Homer Hickam, a middling high school student growing up in West Virginia coal country. After hearing about the first Sputnik launch on the radio, he is inspired to take up rocketry. Motivated to build the best backyard rockets possible, he consequently develops both an interest in and aptitude for subjects like math, chemistry, and physics. His father, John, is a coal miner to the core; he leads strikes and talks passionately about his career's importance to winning the Cold War. John doesn't have much use for Homer's new hobby, but Homer is supported by one of his teachers, Ms. Riley. Homer overcomes a lot of obstacles, including the misgivings of his father, to win a science fair with one of his rockets. He reconciles with his father and goes on to become a rocket scientist as a NASA engineer.

> **October Sky**
>
> **Directed by**
> Joe Johnston
>
> **Cast**
> Jake Gyllenhaal as Homer Hickman, Chris Cooper as John Hickman, Laura Dern as Miss Riley, Chris Owen as Quentin, William Lee Scott as Roy Lee
>
> **Metascore: 71**

Searching for Bobby Fischer is about a boy named Josh who happens upon a chess game in a New York City park. This chance encounter ignites his gift for the game. His father, Fred, takes a while to get his head around his son's talent. There's a great scene in which Fred challenges Josh to a game to gauge his son's ability. After Josh throws the first game (so that he wouldn't hurt his dad's feelings), Josh then effortlessly wins as Fred grinds through every move. In addition to his father, Josh has two mentors. He takes formal lessons from Bruce, a classical chess master whose coaching is designed for success in tournaments. In contrast, Vinnie plays in the parks and he influences Josh with his fast, aggressive, and intimidating style. How Josh grows as a player (and a person), with the support of his father and two mentors, is a fascinating aspect of this movie.

Resiliency Factors

Although Josh from *Searching for Bobby Fischer* seems like a typical, middle-class kid (albeit a phenom at chess), Homer from *October Sky* is an uninspired student heading for an uninspired life following his father's footsteps into the coal industry. But Homer avoids that fate in large part because of his resilient nature. He has to overcome numerous obstacles on his path towards the science fair and, ultimately, Cape Canaveral. Research on resiliency has identified several protective factors, or forces that shield children and young people from the harmful effects of life's obstacles.

One such factor is having a supportive adult.[1] Resiliency theorists have defined the term charismatic adult, who does not necessarily need to be a parent, as someone who fosters resilience by helping kids feel special and appreciated.[2] Successful adults who had learning problems as youngsters have identified the importance of guidance from mentors, teachers, and therapists.[3] Homer's charismatic adult is Ms. Riley, a teacher who sees his potential as a budding engineer. Her faith in him helps him to gain the confidence he needs to persevere, even when his father does not approve of his new-found affinity (at least not at first).

Josh, fortunately, has several charismatic adults in his life, including his father. In a powerful scene one of Josh's teachers questions whether he should devote so much time to chess and Fred vehemently defends him, asserting, "He's better at this than I've ever been at anything in my life. He's better at this than you'll ever be, at anything. My son has a gift. He has a gift, and when you acknowledge that, then maybe we will have something to talk about." Josh's two chess coaches, Bruce and Vinnie, mentor him in their own images (classic chess vs. street chess). But rather than choosing one influence over the other, Josh actually finds a way to meld the two chess styles into a triumphant combination.

Resiliency theories posit that assets can be critical protective factors for students who are suffering from the frustration, disappointment, and self-esteem that so often accompany childhood problems, including learning difficulties. One feature of resilient youngsters is having an interest (like rocketry) or hobby (like chess) that brings comfort when aspects of their lives are in disarray.[4] Such mastery experiences have also been described as "islands of competence".[5] Homer didn't seem to have much going on in

> **SEARCHING FOR BOBBY FISCHER**
>
> **Directed by**
> Steven Zaillian
>
> **Cast**
> Max Pomeranc as Josh Waitzkin, Joe Mantegna as Fred Waitzkin, Joan Allen as Bonnie Waitzkin, Ben Kingsley as Bruce Pandolfini, Laurence Fishburne as Vinnie
>
> **Oscar Nominations**
> Best Cinematography
>
> **Metascore: N/A**

his life to motivate him, certainly regarding school, until the notion of building a rocket got launched in his mind. Josh is much younger than Homer and so had more time to develop affinities, but chess certainly gave his life a direction.

Notes

[1] Werner, E.E., & Smith, R.S. (2001). *Journeys from Childhood to the Midlife: Risk, Resilience, and Recovery.* New York: Cornell University.

[2] Brooks, R., & Goldstein, S. (2004). *The Power of Resilience: Achieving Balance, Confidence, and Personal Strength in Your Life.* New York: McGraw-Hill.

[3] Raskind, M.H., Goldberg, R.J., Higgins, F.L., & Herman, K.L. (1999). Patterns of change and predictors of success in individuals with learning disabilities: Results from a twenty-year longitudinal study. *Learning Disabilities Research and Practice, 14*, 35-49.

[4] Werner, E.E., & Smith, R.S. (1992). *Overcoming the Odds: High Risk Children from Birth to Adulthood.* New York: Cornell University.

[5] Brooks, R., & Goldstein, S. (2001). *Raising Resilient Children: Fostering Strength, Hope, and, Optimism in Your Child.* New York: McGraw-Hill.

Aliens (1986) & 28 Weeks Later (2007)

Whereas the previous chapter discussed how non-parental adults can influence the identity of children, this chapter looks at the reverse- how does assuming a parental role for a child in need change the adult? Obviously, parenthood is a big factor in a person's identity, even for de facto parents.

Mama Bears vs. Monsters

This double-decker thrill ride includes two top-notch sequels to game-changing predecessors. *Aliens* is James Cameron's sequel to *Alien*, Ridley Scott's 1979 masterpiece. *Alien* carved out a whole new niche in sci-fi horror with its intrinsic realism (you can almost smell the grime on the space freighter), quality acting, and shock effects (our chests burst just thinking about them). *28 Weeks Later* is Juan Carlos Fresnadillo's sequel to Danny Boyle's *28 Days Later* (2002), which launched the zombie renaissance (ala, *World War Z*, *The Walking Dead*, *Shaun of the Dead*). Boyle tapped into 20th century fear of apocalyptic plagues and science run amok, and he introduced the elegantly simple innovation of fast-moving zombies.

Aliens and *28 Weeks Later* feature

Aliens

Directed by
James Cameron

Cast
Sigourney Weaver as Ellen Ripley, Carrie Henn as Rebecca 'Newt' Jordan, Michael Biehn as Cpl. Dwayne Hicks, Paul Reiser as Carter Burke, Lance Henriksen as Bishop, Bill Paxton as Pvt. Hudson

Oscar Wins
Best Effects, Sound Effects Editing
Best Effects, Visual Effects

Oscar Nominations
Best Actress in a Leading Role (Sigourney Weaver)
Best Art Direction-Set Decoration
Best Sound
Best Film Editing
Best Music, Original Score

Metascore: 87

military units equipped with fearsome weaponry, technology, and machismo. But up against primal forces (a hive of relentless aliens and hordes of rage virus-infected zombies, respectfully), all that firepower is rendered impotent. In that capacity each film can be viewed as a metaphor for the agonizing military conflicts of their respective eras- *Aliens* and Vietnam, *28 Weeks Later* and the War on Terror (much of *28 Weeks Later* even takes place in a Green Zone).

Both of these movies have strong female leads, such as Helen Ripley in *Aliens*. What makes Ripley so compelling is her emergent maternal instincts and fierce struggle to protect a young girl named Newt, whose family was killed by the aliens. *28 Weeks Later* also uses a child as the "MacGuffin"- Andy is immune to the rage virus so his blood carries a potential cure. He and his older sister are protected by Scarlet, a U.S. Army doctor. Ripley and Scarlet are both supported by studly soldiers with sensitive sides- Hicks in *Aliens* and Doyle in *28 Weeks Later*. Though both Hicks and Doyle get their licks in, ultimately they fall by the wayside as the women soldier on.

Origins of the Maternal Instinct

In both *Aliens* and *28 Weeks Later,* the protagonists become de facto parents as they ferociously defend children in the charge. When mothers safeguard their biological offspring, they are acting to preserve their gene pool. So how do we explain Ripley and Scarlet putting themselves at grave risk for children with whom they share no DNA? Social psychology offers some insight.

Social-exchange theory assumes that helping is motivated by a desire to minimize costs and maximize rewards (both internal and external). That view really challenges the whole notion of altruism and would not explain the incredible costs paid by Ripley and Scarlet in terms of jeopardy to themselves and those around them. However,

Scarlet is acting not only to save Andy, but all of humanity- so her actions are motivated by enormous potential reward. But social-cultural norms can motivate people to help others in an altruistic fashion. For instance, the social-responsibility norm pushes us to help those in need even if they cannot reciprocate. In other words, our cultures deliver the message that helping those in need is simply the right thing to do.

Social psychology research has explored the factors that increase the probability that an individual will help another (even someone who is not a blood-relative). When there are fewer bystanders, we are more likely to notice that someone is in peril, interpret their circumstances as dangerous, and assume responsibility for helping.[1] In both *28 Weeks Later* and *Aliens,* the heroines step up when the biological parents are out of the picture. And as other good guys bite the dust, they ratchet up the heroics. We also are more likely to help those who both need and deserve it and those similar to us.[2] This latter factor relates to Ripley's motives. Having spent decades in suspended animation and losing all those close to her, she naturally would identify with the orphaned Newt (and, of course, both Ripley and Newt survived assaults from the aliens on their own, using only their guts and wits).

> **28 WEEKS LATER**
>
> **Directed by**
> Juan Carlos Fresnadillo
>
> **Cast**
> Robert Carlyle as Don, Rose Byrne as Scarlet, Jeremy Renner as Doyle, Harold Perrineau as Flynn, Catherine McCormack as Alice, Idris Elba as Stone
>
> **Metascore: 78**

Interestingly, *Aliens* concludes with a knock-down, drag-out showdown between Ripley (drawing up every possible ounce of fight from social psychology to defend Newt) and the alien queen (who actually is fighting to protect her own gene pool, monstrous as it is). But is

Ripley fighting an even bigger battle? She mentioned early on how disastrous it would be if even one alien made it to human-occupied territory. So while both she and Scarlett are defending children in the charge over the short-term, critical long-term consequences hang in the balance. That's heroic stuff.

Notes

[1,2] Myers, D.G. (1987). *Social psychology, Second Edition*. New York: McGraw Hill.

The Incredibles (2004) & Hancock (2008)

So we've established that women can assume a maternal role to heroically protect children who are not their own. Next up are a couple of movies that could have been separated at birth because they both pose the same question: What happens when superheroes fall out of favor with society and have to claw their way back into the mainstream as they battle the bad guys? Answering that question will entail looking at the nature of heroism and how it interplays with a person's identity.

With Heroes Like These . . .

The Incredibles is a Disney-Pixar release, but don't let that give the impression that it's a fluffy family picture. In fact, it is rated PG and has a fair amount of violence. Superheroes have been exiled (you know, lawsuits due to collateral damage and such). Mr. Incredible has married Elastigirl, and their family lives under a quasi-witness protection program for former "supers." Mr. Incredible bridles under this forced retirement and longs to get back into the action. He gets his chance when he's lured into trouble by Syndrome, his self-styled nemesis. Elastigirl and her kids, Dash and Violet, have to rescue Dad as they all work together as

---

The Incredibles

Directed by
Brad Bird

Cast
Craig T. Nelson as Bob Parr 'Mr. Incredible', Holly Hunter as Helen Parr 'Elastigirl', Samuel L. Jackson as Lucius Best 'Frozone', Jason Lee as Buddy Pine 'Syndrome', Spencer Fox as Dash Parr, Sarah Vowell as Violet Parr

Oscar Wins
Best Animated Feature Film of the Year
Best Achievement in Sound Editing

Oscar Nominations
Best Writing, Original Screenplay
Best Achievement in Sound Mixing

Metascore: 90

a super-family to save the day. In addition to some great action (Dash's dash through the jungle, pursued by Syndrome's minions, is a showstopper), the movie offers up a lot of fish-out-of-water laughs, like Mom and Dad arguing about the driving route on their way to the showdown with Syndrome, Mom threatening to ground the kids if they don't calm down when their lives are in danger, and Dash tormenting his teacher by placing a tack on his desk chair using his super-speed.

Hancock is the eponymous hero with Superman-like powers of strength, flight, and invulnerability. He also doesn't age, and for decades he has known nothing of his life before an incident in which he sustained a head injury and was abandoned in a hospital (where he was given the generic name, "John Hancock"). The combined effect of amnesia, depression about no one claiming him after his injury, and social isolation have made Hancock an incorrigible drunk. Like the Incredibles, Hancock is an outcast. He sulks, spews profanity, and occasionally steps up to fight crime- usually causing more collateral damage than helping (the opening sequence smash-up of downtown L.A. being a prime example). Enter Ray, a public relations guy who offers to help Hancock rehabilitate his image as payback for saving his life. Ray counsels Hancock in areas such as interacting with law enforcement and costume design. Things get complicated when Hancock and Ray's wife, Mary, realize a connection. Things get even more complicated when that connection affects Hancock's superpowers and capacity to deal with some bad guys.

Heroic Motivations

Heroism is at the heart of this particular double feature. Psychologists have been exploring heroism for decades. Much of the current thinking and research is being driven by Philip Zimbardo, who rose to prominence by examining the roots of evil with his stunning simulated-prison study at Stanford University in the early 1970's.[1] So what, exactly, is heroism? It is a social activity that meets several criteria[2]:

- it is in service to others in need, or in defense of an ideal
- it is a voluntary act
- it is done with a recognition of possible risks/costs
- the hero is willing to accept anticipated sacrifice
- there is no external gain anticipated at the time of the act

Heroism has been analyzed and divided into subtypes. One example is *civil heroism*, which is similar to military heroism in that it involves physical peril except that it does not have a clearly defined code of conduct.[3] Hancock clearly struggles without the guidance that such a code would provide. Rather than falling back on a script, he is left to improvise in his decision-making, with rather mixed results. Another form is *social heroism*, which usually does not involve immediate physical danger, but rather significant risk and sacrifice in other life dimensions, including loss of social status or even ostracism.[4] Given Hancock's and Mr. Incredible's imperviousness, one could argue that they exemplify, in their best moments, social heroism. These superheroes set out to save others from clear and present danger, but they are setting examples and inspiring others. This is part of the message that Ray sends to Hancock. The goal of social heroism really is to preserve a value or standard that is under duress, like a community unraveling.[5] As such, the social hero can be viewed as even more heroic than one engaging in more physical forms of heroism.[6]

The stakes for social heroism get ramped up because of how society treats the hero. In fact, there appears to be an ever-present tension between our desire to revere heroes on the one hand, and to castigate their actions on the other. This fustigation occurs because the actions of social heroes can be viewed as threatening (think of the whistle-blower bringing down a company or industry). But heroes facing physical risk can be seen as threatening as well, especially if they have a checkered history.[7] Hancock and the "supers" from *The Incredibles* got to the point where people feared them because of the collateral damage they could unleash. Envy of superheroes' abilities also contributed to their ostracism, and probably concern about how they up-ended the social order as well (would we need a police force, military, or rescue workers if superheroes were around?).

Motivations of heroes have been explored by psychologists as well. One line of thinking is that the decision to act heroically does not necessarily come from prosocial motivation. Rather, that decision seems to be a private, personal process that occurs before an audience comes into the picture. So the moment of the decision is a lonely one, even if others are present.[8] One of the compelling aspects of both the Incredibles' and Hancock's existences is loneliness. Hancock is utterly alone, a pariah. Though the Incredible family members have each other, they are all struggling with a uniqueness that they cannot express in the workplace, at school, or with other teenagers. In varying ways these superheroes express frustration about being different and the challenges of connecting with others and

---

HANCOCK

Directed by
Peter Berg

Cast
Will Smith as John Hancock, Charlize Theron as Mary, Jason Bateman as Ray, Jae Head as Aaron, Eddie Marsan as Red, David Mattey as Man Mountain, Johnny Galecki as Jeremy

Metascore: 49

society at large (by stories' ends they become a bit more connected, though they're still on their own). The journey of all of these superheroes involves their coming to terms with their abilities and how to use them to protect others and important ideals. They may get some support from non-super types, but they each have to make their own decisions about what kind of people (or super-people) they will be. As Helen tells her kids in *The Incredibles*, "Your identity is your most valuable possession. Protect it."

Notes

[1] Zimbardo, P.G., Haney, C., & Banks, W.C. (1973). A Pirandellian prison. *The New York Times Magazine*, pp. 38-60.

[2,5,8] Franco, Z.E., Blau, K., & Zimbardo, P.G. (2011). Heroism: A Conceptual Analysis and Differentiation Between Heroic Action and Altruism. *Review of General Psychology, 15,* 99-113.

[3] Zimbardo, P.G. (2007). *The Lucifer effect: Understanding how good people turn evil.* New York: Random House.

[4] Glazer, M.P., & Glazer, P.M. (1999). On the trail of courageous behavior. *Sociological Inquiry, 69,* 276–295.

[6] Peterson, C., & Seligman, M.E.P. (2004). *Character strengths and virtues.* Washington, DC: American Psychological Association & Oxford University Press.

[7] Franco, Z., & Zimbardo, P. (2006–07). The banality of heroism. *Greater Good, 3,* 30–35.

Act IV

Emotion Pictures:

Romantic Relationships and Friendships

BLUE VALENTINE (2010) & PRICELESS (2006)

This Act will take us deep into the heart of love, intimacy, and companionship. We start with romantic love from both ends of the tone spectrum- a heavy romantic tragedy and a light romantic comedy.

Comedies, Tragedies, and Other Love Stories

Blue Valentine is about the coming together and falling apart of Dean and Cindy. Through spliced together scenes and timelines, we see the beginning, middle, and end of their relationship. This film manages to capture both the highs (wait for Dean to break out the ukulele) and the lows of their relationship. With remarkable acting and an incredible soundtrack from Grizzly Bear, it is easy to fall in love with the couple- and that's what makes the collapse of the relationship hurt all the more.

Priceless is about the love and misadventures of Irene and Jean who have an unlikely encounter that sparks a complicated. Irene is only interested in seducing rich older men, which Jean is not. Despite Jean's attempts to buy Irene's affection with the little money he does have, he is repeatedly rejected by her. Why? Because she is only interested in financial security, not love. Soon after Irene bleeds him dry, Jean is forced to find a sugar mamma of his own, all while continuing to see Irene as she teaches him the tricks of her trade. This

---

BLUE VALENTINE

Directed by
Derek Cianfrance

Cast
Ryan Gosling as Dean, Michelle Williams as Cindy, Faith Wladyka as Frankie, Mike Vogel as Bobby

Oscar Nominations
Best Performance by an Actress in a Leading Role (Michelle Williams)

Metascore: 81

romantic comedy is clever and charming in a way that only the French can pull off.

While *Priceless* is fun and romantic, *Blue Valentine* is deep and gritty. But each film focuses on a couple figuring out their relationship. What can make watching these two together so interesting is seeing how the characters don't get what they want. In *Priceless*, Irene doesn't want to fall in love with Jean, yet ultimately does. By contrast, *Blue Valentine* has a couple who really love and need each other and desperately want things to work out, and yet their relationship tragically collapses. Get ready to laugh, cry, and marvel at the human chemistry that can unite or divide.

What's Love Got to Do with It?

There is no doubt that romantic love is one of the most interesting and entertaining subjects to explore in films and in the psychological literature. And although the subject of romance is quite diverse, the popular media's portrayal of its features and development is quite narrow. *Priceless* fits the pop culture mold of what romantic love is by the fact that Jean and Irene are young, attractive, intelligent, and in the early stages of their attraction. It's hard to say if our false assumption drives the media or visa-versa but, "Many believe that romantic love is the same as passionate love. It isn't. Romantic love has the intensity, engagement and sexual chemistry that passionate love has, minus the obsessive component. Passionate or obsessive love includes feelings of uncertainty and anxiety. This kind of love helps drive the

> **PRICELESS**
>
> **Directed by**
> Pierre Salvadori
>
> **Cast**
> Audrey Tautou as Irene, Gad Elmaleh as Jean, Marie-Christine Adam as Madeleine, Vernon Dobtcheff as Jacques
>
> **Metascore: 72**

shorter relationships but not the longer ones."[1]

First Jean, and later Irene, have this obsessive quality to their romance, so they would clearly fall into the "passionate love" category. If we were to witness their relationship years after the last scene of them riding off on the scooter, we would see a decrease in their passionate love and what would remain would be up to their collective efforts to grow the romance they had already started to cultivate.

Blue Valentine includes scenes of Dean and Cindy in their passionate love stage, but we also see them struggle to adapt when this passionate love fades away. All couples in long-term relationships face this very real challenge of continuing to grow their bond while adapting to a different emotional fuel source. Although he does seem to be emotionally engaged with his daughter, Dean especially seems to have fallen into a routine and a lack of emotional engagement with Cindy. "Self-expanding theory"[2] holds that couples are more satisfied with their relationship if they engage in novel, challenging, or exciting activities more so than if they just filled their time with routine activities they found to be pleasant or enjoyable.[3] It might be a bit much to attribute all of the dysfunction between Dean and Cindy on the lack of self-expanding activities, but it would be a good start.

It's important to note that many couples become disillusioned with their partner when their passion for each other fades.[4] It seems natural to assume that "we are not in love anymore" because they don't feel the same levels of ecstasy they once did. They incorrectly assume what "normal love" is supposed to be like over time and that if their passion is there at the start, then it should be there to stay. Normal and successful romantic love experiences a shift in its fuel source from passion, which burns hot but is short-lived, to a long and steady companionship romance that warms but may not have the pyrotechnic quality that Hollywood tends to glamorize.[5]

Notes

[1,5] Acevedo, B.P. & Aron, A. (2009). Does a long-term relationship kill romantic love? *Review of General Psychology*, *13*, 59-65.

[2] Aron, A., & Aron, E. (1986). *Love and the expansion of self: Understanding attraction and satisfaction*. New York: Hemisphere.

[3] Aron, A., Norman, C.C., Aron, E.N., McKenna, C., & Heyman, R. (2000) Couples shared participation in novel and arousing activities and experienced relationship quality. *Journal of Personality and Social Psychology*, 78, 273-283.

[4] Muise, A. (2013). *Hot and Heavy or Slow and Steady: Changing Our Perspective on Love.* Retrieved from http://www.scienceofrelationships.com/home/2013/2/20/hot-and-heavy-or-slow-and-steady-changing-our-perspective-on.html

REVOLUTIONARY ROAD (2008) & SCENES FROM A MARRIAGE (1973)

Building from the last chapter about romantic love and how it can shift, we'll now zoom in on romantic love when it encounters troubled waters. According to the scientific literature and our next two films, love does not necessarily conquer all. But it does leave a resounding imprint that endures beyond our expectations. These two films about marriage are separated by an ocean, 35 years, and the Swedish-English language barrier. Both have been praised for their raw honesty and ability to show characters who truly love each other and yet are caught in a seemingly unstoppable unraveling of their relationship.

Untying the Knot

Revolutionary Road introduces us to Frank and April Wheeler, who seem to be living the 1950's American dream. Two thoughtful, attractive people settle down in a beautiful house, he with a stable job, her in the homemaker role, and yet they both find they are very disconnected from their passions (leading lives of "quiet desperation"). The story depicts their desperate and ultimately futile battle against the monotony of their existence.

Scenes from a Marriage tells the story of Johan and Marinne, a seemingly happy and stable couple who gradu-

---

REVOLUNTIONARY ROAD

Directed by
Sam Mendes

Cast
Kate Winslet as April Wheeler, Leonardo DiCaprio as Frank Wheeler

Oscar Nominations
Best Achievement in Art Direction
Best Achievement in Costume Design
Best Performance by an Actor in a Supporting Role (Michael Shannon)

Golden Globe Wins
Best Performance by an Actress in a Motion Picture - Drama (Kate Winslet)

Metascore: 69

ally realize, like Frank and April, that they are quite unhappy. Even after their marriage deteriorates, they are drawn back to each other. They come to realize that despite being unable to live with each other, they are also unable to live without each other.

The Distance between Two People

In the early stages of marriage there are certain behaviors that are high predictors of divorce. These have been deemed, "The Four Horsemen of the Apocalypse"[1] and are:

- Criticism

- Contempt

- Defensiveness

- Stonewalling

Criticism and defensiveness certainly show up for Jack and April. Johan and Marinne's symptoms are more pronounced later in the relationship but we see the foreshadowing of contempt during their very awkward dinner with friends who display the full-grown version. One caveat in applying the four horsemen for these couples is that the research looks for the early signs within the marriage. We see Johan and Marinne's relationship from year 10 through 30 and so their patterns are much more established.

It might seem more appropriate to rename *Scenes from a Marriage* as "Scenes from a Relationship" since throughout their 30 years, Johan and Marinne go from being married to divorced, then reconnected, and later have an affair with each other even though they both have remarried. It also could have been called "Scenes from an Attachment" since the characters seem to have this un-severable connection, even when physically and legally separated. Oxytocin is the attachment hormone that our bodies release to bond two people. Just as parents and children experience attachment to each other at birth, during breastfeeding and extended physical contact, couples experience attachment through sexual contact.[2] The theme of lasting attachment despite a volatile and sometimes violent interpersonal behavior is evident with both couples. We see them have shockingly destructive fights (especially Jack and April) and then reunite in waves of passion.

So if our couples are so bonded, what went wrong? At year 10, Johan and Marinne appear to have settled into marriage and are happy, albeit a bit complacent. Marinne makes small remarks about unfulfilled hopes and eventually Johan has an affair. It's a no-brainer that infidelity wreaks havoc on a marriage but it's less clear what patterns lead up to the infidelity. Research looked into remedies for founding marriages, some of which have been titled, "The Seven Principles for Making Marriage Work"[3]:

- enhancing love maps

- nurturing fondness and admiration

- turning toward each other

- accepting influence

- solving solvable problems

- overcoming gridlock

- creating shared meaning

Accepting influence- or yielding to each other- would benefit both couples. Instead of an endless cycle of vitriol, Jack and April could jumpstart a positive trend by listening to the other and following through with the other's needs (as opposed to their own demands). If Jack focused his energy on listening to April, his requests and needs would likely be honored by her once she experienced his responsiveness. Both couples need to accept the differences that lie between them and find ways to navigate around them rather than attacking or ignoring them. So Marinne might have to

> **SCENES FROM A MARRIAGE**
>
> **Directed by**
> Ingmar Bergman
>
> **Cast**
> Liv Ullmann as Marianne, Eerland Josephson as Johan, Gunnel Lindblom as Eva
>
> **Golden Globe Wins**
> Best Foreign Film
>
> **Metascore: N/A**

accept parts of Johan's insecurity as a permanent aspect of their relationship; the more she tries to change him or avoid him when he embodies these traits, the more they lead parallel lives. We see the implosion of Jack and April's relationship when he doesn't honor her dream to move to Paris. Europe may not be the answer to all their problems, but acknowledging April's dream is a vital part of how Jack can overcome gridlock. Finally, these couples need to create shared meaning. They have been sliding slowly and steadily into lives of quiet desperation. In the beginning of their marriages, their lives were charming and comfortable. But when they have comfort without substance, they falter. Moving to Paris or having a child might have been the shared purpose Jack and April needed, but as we saw with Johan and Marinne's marriage, children or a relocation does not necessarily build meaning. Much like individual happiness, comfort in a marriage should not be an objective in and of itself- it must a byproduct of striving for and achieving a meaningful goal.

Notes

[1] Gottman, J. (1994). *Why marriages succeed or fail.* New York: Simon &

Schuster.

[2] Schneiderman, I., Zagoory-Sharon, O., Leckman, J.F., & Feldman, R. (2012). Oxytocin during the initial stages of romantic attachment: Relations to couples' interactive reciprocity. *Psychoneuroendocrinology, 37*, 1277–1285.

[3] Gottman, J. & Silver, N. (1999). *The seven principles for making marriage work: A practical guide from the country's foremost relationship expert.* New York: Three Rivers.

Say Anything (1989) & Garden State (2004)

The last couple of chapters have traversed some intense territory about love and relationships. Now we'll look at love's healing power. The next two movies offer nostalgic cultural appeal, including music that is tied in seamlessly with the storylines.

The Soundtrack of Our Lives

Say Anything is a very well-crafted romantic comedy about Lloyd, a high school graduate who falls in love with Diane, the drop-dead valedictorian who is way out of his league. *Garden State* is a quirky coming of age tale about Andrew, a dazed and confused actor who learns what it means to live life with spontaneity and uniqueness from Sam, a young woman who drops into his life. These movies are about young characters who are, in varying ways, lost. They are aimless professionally and in terms of romantic relationships. Bonds with parents are either damaged or severed. Lloyd and Andrew, put simply, are failing to launch. Even Diane, the superstar student with a bright academic future, is thrown for a loop by the incarceration of her father.

Both movies boast memorable and well-integrated soundtracks. *Say Anything* has an iconic scene with Peter Gabriel's classic "In Your Eyes." Lloyd, desperate to win back Diane after she dumped him, plays there song

> **SAY ANYTHING**
>
> **Directed by**
> Cameron Crowe
>
> **Cast**
> John Cusack as Lloyd Dobler, Ione Skye as Diane Court, John Mahoney as James Court, Lili Taylor as Corey Flood, Amy Brooks as D.C., Pamela Adlon as Rebecca, Jeremy Pivon as Mark
>
> **Metascore: 86**

outside her home. In *Garden State*, when Sam and Andrew meet he asks what she is listening to on her headphones. She answers, "The Shins," followed by her plug that "They will change your life." Andrew listens and has a moment when the music syncs up perfectly with Sam's smile- and therein lies the small beginning of a monumental change in his life. These films utilize music not just as filler or background, but as drivers of the stories.

Both films have very believable characters with quirks and uniqueness that show themselves naturally throughout the films. In *Say Anything*, they come alive though their sometimes awkward but exhilarating love for each other. For *Garden State*, they share an existential experience while wearing trash bags in the rain, staring down a bottomless pit, and screaming into the void.

This is Your Mind on Love

Again, each of the protagonists in these films is a mess. *Say Anything*'s Lloyd is a high school wallflower whose ambitions seem to be limited to the nascent sport of kick-boxing (mixed martial arts had yet to erupt in 1989). *Garden State*'s Andrew is a neurotic actor with little success (he has to wait tables to make ends meet) and is so over-medicated that he lives life in a stupor- protected from emotional pain, but numb to anything positive. But each of these guys is shaken loose by that time-honored tonic- the love of a good woman.

Diane gives Lloyd's life purpose, in a rather literal sense. When grilled by her father about what he plans to do with his post-high school future, he responds that his goal is to spend as much time as humanly possible with Diane (which, admittedly, could be a recipe for co-dependence). Later he adds that he is "good at" being with her. And the movie ends with Lloyd joining Diane on her European adventure. She's off to make the world a better place and his role is to make her world a better place.

Whereas Diane is Lloyd's beacon, Andrew goes through a transformation for a variety of reasons, such as the death of his mother, getting off his medication, and his friendship with Mark. But his romance with Sam is a big factor. She gives his life a jolt of, well ... life. She is a free-thinker who works moments of originality into her everyday existence. While it might be a stretch to say that her spunkiness rubs off on him, she animates him enough to start facing some demons, and to yell into the abyss (literally).

> **GARDEN STATE**
>
> **Directed by**
> Zach Braff
>
> **Cast**
> Zach Braff as Andrew Largeman, Natalie Portman as Sam, Ian Holm as Gideon Largeman, Peter Sarsgaard as Mark, Jackie Hoffman as Aunt Sylvia Largeman, Ron Leibman as Dr. Cohen
>
> **Metascore: 67**

Lloyd's and Andrew's progressions are consistent with psychological theory. Exploring current relationships can bring about changes in internal working models of one's self or how a person views him/herself in relation to the world.[1] Attachment theory considers the quality of connections between a person and significant others, starting early in life between a child and parents. One study based on attachment theory looked at the romantic relationships and well-being of close to 500 students, ages 17-21 years. That study found that individuals who had secure romantic attachments were less stressed and lonely, as well as more gratified from an academic standpoint, than those with less positive attachments, including clingy or casual/fickle relationships. These findings were independent of current relationship status, meaning that the positive benefits of a positive relationship last after a break-up.[2]

So we have research to back up the notion that the

love of a good man or woman is powerful medicine. That medicine can act in various ways, though. Diane gives Lloyd must needed focus; with her he can plot a course through life. Sam does the opposite for Andrew; she helps him turn off the auto-pilot. He needed to break free of his existence and at the end he asks her, almost with relief, what they should do next.

Notes

[1] Dozier, M., & Tyrrell, C. (1998). The role of attachment in therapeutic relationships. In J.A. Simpson & W.S. Rholes (Eds.). *Attachment Theory and Close Relationships* (pp. 221-248). New York: Guilford.

[2] Moore, S., & Leung, C. (2002). Young people's romantic attachment styles and their associations with well-being. *Journal of Adolescence, 25,* 243-255.

CinemAnalysis

Waitress (2007) & Like Water for Chocolate (1992)

So now we know that love is good medicine. But what fuels love? Well, one ingredient is more obvious than you might think... This double feature will get your stomach rumbling with delicious food imagery. But, more importantly, these flicks offer plenty of food for thought about womanhood, attraction, and love.

Cookin' Up Some Love

Waitress is about Jenna, a diner waitress with a gift for baking pies. It's a serious gift and she often loses herself in her recipe ideas to escape from her marriage to the appalling Earl. Jenna gets pregnant and dreads the thought of motherhood (at least with Earl's child). She starts an affair with her married doctor, Jim. Jenna's maternal instincts don't kick in until she gives birth to her daughter; in the delivery room she simultaneously falls in love with her child and kicks Earl to the curb. Bucking Hollywood norms, however, Jenna doesn't run to Jim (their affair just helped Jenna break from Earl). She opens her own diner, where she can share her pies with the world, and she and her daughter walk off into the sunset.

Like Water for Chocolate is the story of Tita. She falls in love with Pedro, but is forbidden to marry him because her mother insists that the oldest daughter marry first and that Tita should take care of her mother. Tita's

Waitress

Directed by
Adrienne Shelly

Cast
Keri Russell as Jenna Hunterson, Nathan Fillion as Dr. Jim Pomatter, Cheryl Hines as Becky, Jeremy Sisto as Earl Hunterson, Andy Griffith as Old Joe, Adrienne Shelly as Dawn

Metascore: 75

culinary talents veer into the mystical. For example, when Tita is forced to cook at the wedding of Pedro and her sister, she pours her desire for Pedro into her cooking and the wedding guests are intoxicated with a longing for their true love. By cooking quail with rose petals, she creates a powerful aphrodisiac (so powerful, in fact, that one diner's body heat sets a building on fire). Despite significant familial and social obstacles, Tita maintains her love for Pedro until their deaths.

Waitress is a relatively grounded film that only gets surreal when Jenna ponders new pie recipes. In contrast, *Like Water for Chocolate* has so many surreal elements that it's like a fantasy - an allegory about the struggle to find true love. Both will make your mouth water.

The Science of Sensuality

So is there any science behind the myth that foods can be aphrodisiacs? Actually, there is a fair amount of research supporting this. Several foods have been found to be particularly enticing during the flirting phase, such as chili peppers (spiciness gets the heart pounding and induce sweating) and bananas, which have a mood-lifting quality for increased confidence (Warner, 2005). Food preparation can be a form of foreplay, or simply romantic connection. *Waitress* has a tender and sensual scene in which Jenna invites Jim into her kitchen to share some of her pie-making secrets.

Some foods promote seduction, such as by triggering the release of sex hormones like tes-

---

LIKE WATER FOR CHOCOLATE

Directed by
Alfonso Arau

Cast
Marco Leonardi as Pedro Muzquiz, Lumi Cavazos as Tita, Regina Torné as Mama Elena, Mario Iván Martínez as Dr. John Brown, Ada Carrasco as Nacha

Metascore: N/A

tosterone, providing an energy boost, or increasing blood flow to the genitals (wow!). Also, the iodine in shrimp stimulates the thyroid gland for energy. The appearance of food also plays a part in its aphrodisiac quality (curves, smooth textures, warm colors, etc.). Some foods are even thought to improve sexual performance. Foods like cheese pizza, buttered popcorn, and pumpkin pie increase penile blood flow. In fact, such foods get the blood flowing down there even better than floral perfume. Believe it or not, but the combination of "Good and Plenty" candy and cucumber was the most potent sexual scent in terms of increasing blood flow to the vaginal area.[1] And what about the most mythical aphrodisiac of all? Chocolate has been reported to release phenylethylamine and serotonin into the human system, producing some aphrodisiac and mood-lifting effects.[2]

Attraction, sex, and bliss set the table for loving and being loved. In the next chapter, we diverge from romantic and sexual connection to the less glamorized but still profound connection between intimate friends.

Notes

[1] Warner, J. (2005). *Eat Your Way to a Spicier Sex Life*. Retrieved from http://www.medicinenet.com/script/main/art.asp?articlekey=52375.

[2] Afoakwa, E.O. (2008). Cocoa and chocolate consumption – Are there aphrodisiac and other benefits for human health? *South African Journal of Clinical Nutrition, 21*, 107-113.

Lost in Translation (2003) & The Station Agent (2003)

Those of us who are lucky enough to have a best friend know how important this kind of relationship can be. Most people want a fellow traveler with whom to walk on life's journey. This chapter showcases two great indie films that have much more in common than just their year of release. Both have simple, character-driven stories that imply much more than they state overtly. They require the audience to perceive and think about the characters, and yet the films don't come off as especially cerebral.

Kindred Spirits

In *The Station Agent* we meet Fin, a lonely man, born with dwarfism, who has a passion for locomotives. He reluctantly meets and becomes friends with two other forlorn souls, Henry and Olivia. Together they form a friendship that is genuine and adventurous. One could argue that aside from their loneliness, each of these three central characters could not be more different. Although they each have their struggles and feelings of emptiness, these friendships do not turn into a help-me-and-I'll-help-you dynamic. They simply spend time together and it brings them life.

Lost in Translation

Directed by
Sofia Coppola

Cast
Scarlett Johansson as Charlotte, Bill Murray as Bob Harris, Giovanni Ribisi as John, Anna Faris as Kelly

Oscar Wins
Best Writing, Original Screenplay

Oscar Nominations
Best Picture
Best Actor in a Leading Role (Bill Murray)
Best Director

Golden Globe Wins
Best Motion Picture – Comedy or Musical
Best Performance by an Actor in a Motion Picture – Comedy or Musical (Bill Murray)
Best Screenplay – Motion Picture

Metascore: 89

This same kind of reinvigoration takes place in *Lost in Translation*. Bob is a famous actor sent to Tokyo to shoot a commercial. Charlotte is the new wife of an eccentric photographer also in Tokyo because she didn't know what else to do. Bob and Charlotte are two very different people in different life stages. But they both are lonely and lacking in purpose. They meet and become friends (almost lovers), in large part because they are fish out of water in the unique culture of Tokyo. It may be hard to pinpoint what resonates about *Lost in Translation*, but at the heart of the story is a magical, heart-aching connection between Bob and Charlotte. They can't end up together, but without even trying they help each other along on their journeys.

> **THE STATION AGENT**
>
> **Directed by**
> Thomas McCarthy
>
> **Cast**
> Peter Dinklage as Finbar McBride, Paul Benjamin as Henry Styles, Bobby Cannavale as Joe Oramas, Patricia Clarkson as Olivia Harris, Michelle Williams as Emily, John Slattery as David
>
> **Metascore: 81**

Take Two Friendships and Call Me in the Morning

Medication and psychotherapy are the standard course for individuals experiencing mood disorders like depression. But any competent clinician will use additional mood-boosting strategies as well. The truth is that regular exercise and spending time with friends have each been shown repeatedly to be effective at improving mood.[1] The power of friendship is on full display in these two films. The bond Fin forms with Henry and Olivia is simple but genuine. It's clear the Fin is much better off by the end of the film and what's noteworthy is that he doesn't confess a deep secret or have an epiphany about his life- he just spends time with people who allow him to be himself.

Bob and Charlotte have conversations that are more

insight-oriented, such as Bob giving advice about how age makes it easier to handle disappointment. But here again is where friendship can be so powerful. Through their time together, they form trust, and from the trust comes honesty about their disillusionment. When friends have the courage and wisdom to walk with each other through difficult circumstances, they often offer advice and encouragement in much the same way a therapist does.[2] Bob and Charlotte are much more whole after their week together. Even though they may not have been looking for it, their friendship made a positive difference.

When we strip away the roles that come along with romantic, parental, and family relationships, we are left with friendship. Being friends might the closest we get to an agenda-free relationship. It can be a connection that is less about what you can do or who you can become and more about *who you are*. And that's just what the doctor ordered for the characters in these films.

Notes

[1] Waterhouse, B., & O'Connor, R.J. (2009). Care by companionship – a proposal for prescription friends. *Journal of The Royal Society of Medicine, 102,* 504.

[2] Ernst, J.M., & Cacioppo, J.T. (1998). Lonely hearts: Psychological perspectives on loneliness. *Applied and Preventive Psychology, 8,* 1–22.

Act V

Streaming Consciousness:

Cognition & Perception in Movies

CinemAnalysis

Pan's Labyrinth (2006) & The Fall (2006)

In this penultimate Act we explore some abstract aspects of the psychological landscape: consciousness, cognition, and perception. To be sure, the world in between our ears can be vivid. This first chapter explores how a child's use of fantasy can actually be adaptive. While kids are not good at being adults, they are very skilled at being children. They are understanding, perceiving and gleaning in ways that often go unnoticed. These two stunning films were produced the same year and have their own take on wonder and fantasy. In each the protagonist is a young girl who uses imagination for escapism. However, both find that the world of fantasy can be just as fearsome and harsh as the reality they are trying to escape.

Dreamscape Escapes

Pan's Labyrinth tells the story of Ofelia, who travels with her pregnant mother to live with her merciless step-father in post-civil war Spain. As Ofelia's situation seems increasingly hopeless, she escapes her life though secret passages of fantasy and fairy tales. A faun tells her she is the Princess Moanna - the king of the underworld's daughter. He adds that in order for her to prove herself as the princess, she must complete three increasingly daunting tests before the full moon and then she will be reunited with

Pan's Labyrinth

Directed by
Guillermo del Toro

Cast
Ivana Baquero as Ofelia, Sergi Lopéz as Vidal, Maribel Verdú as Mercedes, Doug Jones as Fauno, Ariadna Gil as Carmen, Álex Angulo as Dr. Ferreiro

Oscar Wins
Best Achievement in Art Direction
Best Achievement in Cinematography
Best Achievement in Makeup

Oscar Nominations
Best Achievement in Music Written for Motion Pictures, Original Score
Best Foreign Language Film of the Year
Best Writing, Original Screenplay

Metascore: 98

her real father. First, she must steal a key from the belly of a giant toad. Second, she is to retrieve a dagger from the lair of a child eating demon. And her third test will be the most demanding of all- sacrifice her newly born baby brother, now her only surviving family member.

The Fall was set in 1920's Hollywood and introduces Roy, a stunt man who has suffered a fall that may leave him paralyzed. In the hospital, Roy meets and becomes friends with Alexandra, a girl who has broken her arm. Roy tells a story about six characters who are on a mission to kill an evil governor. Roy's narration is accompanied by images from Alexandra's mind as she processes his stories. The world Alexandra creates has to be seen to be believed. Director Tarsem Singh spent millions of his own money to create a visual masterpiece with extraordinary colors, textures and contrasts, including footage from 28 countries- all without computer-generated imagery.

For all the similarities of these two films, they each have a different feel to them. *Pan's Labyrinth* is a much darker and fearsome while *The Fall* becomes edgier as the truth of the grownup world becomes revealed to Alexandra. But both of these films showcase how vivid and powerful imagination can be.

Solving Real-Life Problems through Magical Thinking

Solving a problem through fantasy may not sound like solving a problem at all. It's tempting to see imagination as what children do for fun and therefore not useful for dealing with real world problems. But developmental psychologists Jean Piaget and Erik Erikson hold that imagination is a highly sophisticated method for self-teaching.[1] Imagination and knowledge interplay in important ways. In her book, *The Philosophical Baby*, Alison Gopnik keenly points out that, "Knowledge is actually what gives imagination its power, what makes creativity possible. It's because we know about the world that we can create possible worlds."[2] In this way, an individual (not just a child) can create an imaginary stage where scenarios are played out and interacted with for a purpose.

In *Pan's Labyrinth* Ofelia is quite powerless to stop her evil stepfather's reign of terror, much less assist the rebels against him. She needs an escape route, which the faun offers. But her anxiety only increases when he explains that she must sacrifice her baby brother. Nothing about Ophelia's circumstances is easy, whether in the real world or the fantasy: escaping giant monsters and deciphering the trustworthiness of a faun vs. escaping an evil and powerful stepfather. The audience has a bird's eye view of her dual existence in real and fantasy worlds. Ophelia's fantasy labyrinth is her way of calculating how and when she will run away in the real world. As dark as her imaginary world is, her fantasy gives her the idealistic notion that she is a princess returning home to a loving father. She does not have much hope in the real world, so her optimism flows from her imagination. Without hope, she would be hard-pressed to summon the courage to escape her stepfather.

> **THE FALL**
>
> **Directed by**
> Tarsem Singh
>
> **Cast**
> Catinca Untaru as Alexandria, Justine Waddell as Nurse Evelyn, Lee Pace as Roy Walker, Sean Gilder as Walt Purdy
>
> **Metascore: 64**

One study revealed some interesting things about the link between imagination and optimism. Researchers asked 162 children, ages 9 to 15, to write about life events as well as future events they expected for themselves. They arrived at two interesting conclusions. First, children told more cohesive stories about their imagined futures than their real pasts. Second, the biographical stories included negative past events, yet the perceived future lives were mostly positive.[3] That research supports the notion that imagination aids a child's sense of optimism. This is in line with other research showing that optimism, in reasonable doses, is a strength and aids a child's resiliency.[4]

In *The Fall* Roy is without hope. He uses his story as a ploy for Alexandra to get him morphine pills so he can end his own life. When his plan fails, Alexandra demands that he finish the story. Roy attempts to finish the story but concocts a tragedy. This lack of hope is unacceptable to Alexandra and she insists that there be some optimism. In the end, the characters that represent her and Roy are heroes that emerge from the ashes, able to fight another day. The film mimics this same process as Roy regains use of his legs. Alexandra's arm also recovers, and she is reunited with her family. Roy, like many adults, might struggle with the disappointing past and present. What he needed was a good dose of childlike fantasy in order to find solutions, patience, and hope. Narratives like *Pan's Labyrinth* and *The Fall* are compelling partly because they convey what research has uncovered- hope is perhaps best manufactured through imagination.

Notes

[1] Frost, J.L., Wortham, S.C., & Reifel, S. (2007). *Play and social-emotional development.* New York: Pearson Education.

[2] Gopnik, A. (2009). *The philosophical baby.* New York: Picador Reading Group.

[3] Bohn, A., & Berntsen, D. (2013). The future is bright and predictable: The development of prospective life stories across childhood and adolescence. *Developmental Psychology, 49,* 1232-1241.

[4] Seligman, M. (1995). *The optimistic child: A proven program to safeguard children against depression and build lifelong resilience.* New York: Houghton Mifflin Harcourt.

INCEPTION (2010) & WAKING LIFE (2001)

Having just discussed how children use imagination, let's now discuss the unreal world of dreams. These next two films provide a strong reference for questions about what it means to be conscious by showing characters who are both lucid and unconscious. Lucid dreaming offers a special kind of paradox because the dreamer experiences themselves as being in that state, though not entirely. Technically speaking, nothing in the lucid dream is real (in the sense that the person is not interacting with physical matter), yet the psychological experience is very real. So keep an open mind about what this all means and let the films and scientific research fuel your curiosity.

A Dream of a Double-Feature

Inception is a tour-de-force that offers just about everything one could want from a summer blockbuster: great action, stunning visuals, compelling acting, and a storyline that is as original as it is thought-provoking. *Waking Life* offers much of the same creativity, also with a dream-within-a-dream premise, and yet provides a very different viewing experience.

Inception begins with Cobb, a unique kind of thief who enters the dreams of a person and extracts valuable information from his or her subconscious. While the premise might sound similar to other films such as *The Cell* (2000), *Inception* gives us another layer to chew on by introducing the possibility of a dream-within-a-dream-(within-a-dream, etc.). Though the story gets complicated, following along actually isn't too difficult. Rules of meta-dreams are introduced, such as the depth of the dream having an expanding effect on time and the mind's propensity to fight off interlopers. Such rules actually make the experience more exhilarating because they push the characters through the story (rolling one dreamer's inner ear is how the famous spinning hallway fight sequence came to be).

Waking Life has a unique premise but also a unique esthetic due to the use of rotoscoping, a technique in which animators draw over live action footage. The effect puts one foot in reality and one foot out, since motion looks real while the layered color pulls the viewer into a fantasy world. *Waking Life* begins with a young man who is on a journey of some kind. He has conversations with a variety of characters, all passionately explaining their ideas of the meaning of life, the universe, and the mystery of dreams. Each conversation ends with his waking and realizing that the previous conversation had been a dream. Shortly after, he has another encounter that also proves to be a dream. Eventually the young man wonders if he will ever completely awake. Incidentally, the term "waking life" refers to a moment when one wakes from a dream and the "real" world seems more unbelievable than the fantasy world one just departed.

Both films try to get their arms around the dream experience. *Inception*, especially, works to explain the machinations of dreams, to put some order to the chaos. At the same time, these films respect the mystery and

> **INCEPTION**
>
> **Directed by**
> Christopher Nolan
>
> **Cast**
> Leonardo Dicaprio as Cobb, Joseph Gordon-Levitt as Arthur, Ellen Page as Ariadne, Tom Hardy as Eames, Ken Watanbe as Saito, Marion Cotillard as Mal, Michael Caine as Miles
>
> **Oscar Wins**
> Best Achievement in Cinematography
> Best Achievement in Sound Editing
> Best Achievements in Sound Mixing
> Best Achievement in Visual Effects
>
> **Oscar Nominations**
> Best Motion Picture of the Year
> Best Achievement Art Direction
> Best Writing, Original Screenplay
> Best Achievement in Music Written for Motion Pictures, Original Score
>
> **Metascore: 74**

feed the imagination with endless possibilities that dream worlds offer.

The Science of Dreaming

It's pretty hard to talk about psychology and dreams without evoking psychoanalysts Sigmund Freud and Carl Jung. Freud considered dreams "the royal road to the unconscious".[1] He believed that the patient's dreams expressed their neuroticism in a disguised fashion. Tell Freud you had a dream about hotdogs, skyscrapers, or telephone poles, and he would likely interpret these symbols as your preoccupation with male anatomy. He believed that dreams disguised the disturbing fixations of our most basic, instinctual drives because the truth was too difficult to accept on a conscious level.

Jung, on the other hand, had even higher respect for the insight of dreams. He believed, like Freud, that dreams involved symbols from the subconscious; but, unlike Freud, he urged his patients to uncover the wisdom that the subconscious was trying to communicate to the conscious self. In other words, for Jung the subconscious offered something more profound, while Freud thought it consisted of more primitive, animalistic urges.[2]

But psychoanalysts are not alone in their high regard for the power of dreams. In recent years neuroscience has exploded with new and fascinating descriptions of how sleep and dreams affect our waking life and consolidate learning. One study showed that subjects tested best on visual

> **WAKING LIFE**
>
> **Directed by**
> Richard Linklater
>
> **Cast**
> Trevor Jack Brooks as Young Boy, Lorelei Linklater as Young Girl, Wiley Wiggins as Main Character, Glover Gill as Accordion Player, Lara Hicks as Violin Player
>
> **Metascore: 82**

discrimination (differentiating targets like symbols or shapes) 48-96 hours after their initial training even though they received no further practice. The 2-4 days of sleep in between training and testing enabled optimal performance on this kind of learning task.[3]

Interestingly, a growing field called neuropsychoanalysis is full of prominent researchers who believe that Freud was not too far off in his model of dreams and the mind. Antonio Dames, Head of Neurology at the University of Iowa College of Medicine, asserts that "Freud's insights on the nature of consciousness are consonant with the most advanced contemporary neuroscience views".[4] Not bad for an Austrian neurologist working in the early 20th century without a brain scanner in sight. For better or worse, Freud's relevance in modern psychology looks to be with us for the foreseeable future.

Inception gives a rich metaphor of the subconscious when Cobb takes a rickety old elevator down to the basement of his mind where he holds memories and the persona of his deceased wife, Mal. Despite his efforts to suppress her, she has become an increasingly powerful and destructive force in his mind. She distracts, taunts, and confuses him when his resolve is most tested. Likewise, *Waking Life's* filming techniques capture the visible metamorphosis that can take place in dreams as meaning changes the perception, such as the rant by Alex Jones where he becomes more and more red the madder he gets. What might be considered a static object in the real world is often ever-changing in dreams because the more we understand and perceive an object, the more the object in question changes. In their own ways, these films play with the psychoanalytic notion of dreams as compact metaphors of the human experience.

Notes

[1] Freud, S. (1913). *The Interpretation of Dreams*. New York: Macmillan.

[2] Jung, C.G. (1995*). Modern Man In Search of a Soul.* (C.F. Baynes & W.S. Dell, Trans.) New York: Houghton Mifflin Harcourt.

[3] Stickgold, R. & LaTanya, J. (2000). Visual discrimination learning requires sleep after training. *Nature Neuroscience, 3,* 1237-1238.

[4] Guterl, F. (2002, Nov 10). What Freud Got Right. *Newsweek Magazine*. Retrieved from http://www.thedailybeast.com/newsweek/2002/11/10/what-freud-got-right.html.

Eternal Sunshine of the Spotless Mind (2004) & Vanilla Sky (2001)

The experience of recalling experiences and sensations can be wonderful and, at times, painful. These next two films explore what would happen if eradicating painful memories were possible. By asserting that such an endeavor would be fraught with problems, they illustrate that it might just be untenable to amputate the past and yet remain whole as a person.

I'll Take Reality, Thank You Very Much

Eternal Sunshine of the Spotless Mind is the brainchild of Charlie Kaufman, the screenwriter of the wildly creative *Being John Malkovich* (1999). He throws us into the story of Joel Barish, whose life seems to be depressive and strangely disconnected. His confusion is due to a procedure he has undergone to erase all memory of his former girlfriend, Clementine, who has undergone the same procedure to erase him from her memory. As Joel puts together the pieces of why and how this has happened, the narrative of his memories is depicted in lucid-like dreams. Regretting his decision, Joel desperately navigates his mind to stop the mental eradication of the woman he still loves. He even enlists the help of Clementine's memory, who

> **ETERNAL SUNSHINE OF THE SPOTLESS MIND**
>
> **Directed by**
> Michel Gondry
>
> **Cast**
> Jim Carrey as Joel Barish, Kate Winslet as Clementine Krucynski, Elijah Wood as Patrick, Thomas Jay Ryan as Frank, Mark Ruffalo as Stan, Kirsten Dunst as Mary, Jane Adams as Carrie, Tom Wilkinson as Dr. Mierzwiak
>
> **Oscar Wins**
> Best Writing, Original Screenplay
>
> **Oscar Nominations**
> Best Performance by an Actress in a Leading Role (Kate Winslet)
>
> **Metascore:** 89

becomes a kind of cognitive sidekick.

Based on the Spanish film *Open Your Eyes* (1997), *Vanilla Sky* takes us on a similar journey. The dreamy protagonist is the handsome and brash David. In contrast to *Eternal Sunshine of the Spotless Mind*, our understanding of David's dream state is not revealed until the end of the film when his tender romance with Sophia turns into a nightmare: David has chosen to exist in a perpetual, lucid dream so that he can live his wished-for life without the facial disfigurement he incurred soon after meeting Sophia in real life.

Both of these films show characters living in altered realities of their own choosing. Yet when their cognitive veil is pulled to the side, they long for their authentic existences where they face the problems they desperately wanted to forget. This theme is explored in other movies like *The Truman Show* (1998) and *The Matrix* (1999). Is the message that masochism is preferable to numbing escapism? Certainly it's more nuanced than that. For all our faults, humans are disposed to accept pain, confusion, and disappointment for the sake of something bigger or better. Put simply, we don't always want the easy road.

Memories and Psychotherapy

Both of these movies push the idea that forgetting can be therapeutic, at least up to a point. *Eternal Sunshine of the Spotless Mind* is about out-and-out memory erasure. *Vanilla Sky* combines memory wiping of a traumatic event with the insertion of new, artificial memories. In contrast, psychotherapy usually involves remembering- either recalling repressed experiences or developing mechanisms for better handling traumatic memories. Psychoanalytic theories put a lot of stock in the culling of memories. Carl Jung wrote about archetypes, which are primordial images akin to cultural motifs, which contribute to our collective unconscious or shared memories (think of the shadowy, evil figure). Contemplating the presence or absence of archetypes was thought to be therapeutic by Jung and other psychoanalysts.[1] Some archetypes pop up in these movies, like the father-figure David encounters in *Vanilla Sky* and the child-figure in *Eternal Sunshine of the Spotless Mind* that Clementine assumes when she slips into Joel's early memories.

Abreaction refers to the therapist's urging the patient to remember something, perhaps aided through hypnosis. Sigmund Freud though that this process was the mechanism for the cure of symptoms in the cathartic method.[2] Both Joel and David experience a flood of real memories at the end of their stories, and those catharses actually turned out to be more therapeutic than the systematic forgetting they had undergone.

A central tenet of clinical pathology is that some memories are dysfunctional and that therapeutic change results from the processing of such memories within larger adaptive mental networks. Eye movement desensitization and reprocessing (EMDR) is a therapy used to ameliorate the effects of traumatic memories, relapse triggers, and physical cravings.[3] EMDR involves leading client recollections of disturbing events along with sets of eye movements, and then replacing negative beliefs about the events (such as, "I was powerless.") with positive beliefs (like, "Now I am in control.").[4] In contrast to extinction-based exposure therapies,

> **VANILLA SKY**
>
> **Directed by**
> Cameron Crowe
>
> **Cast**
> Tom Cruise as David Aames, Penélope Cruz as Sofia Serrano, Cameron Diaz as Julie Gianni, Kurt Russell as McCabe, Jason Lee as Brian Shelby, Noah Taylor as Edmund Venturea, Timothy Spall as Thomas Tipp, Johnny Galecki as Peter Brown, Conan O'Brien as himself
>
> **Oscar Nominations**
> Best Music, Original Song ("Vanilla Sky")
>
> **Metascore: 45**

memories targeted through EMDR are thought to be transformed by the therapy and then reconsolidated[5]; the EMDR patient is encouraged to remember, and then the nature of those memories are, in a sense, calmed.

In exposure therapy the therapist identifies the memories, emotions, and physiological arousals that accompany a fear-inducing stimulus and then works to break the pattern of escape that strengthens the fear response. This is accomplished through measured exposure to progressively stronger stimuli until habituation is achieved, or the client is no longer negatively affected by the stimuli.[6]

So how fictional are the science-fictional ideas depicted in *Eternal Sunshine of the Spotless Mind* and *Vanilla Sky*? Virtual reality exposure (VRE) therapy is a relatively new development in the treatment of posttraumatic stress disorder (PTSD). It has been tested on several active duty Army soldiers using an immersive computer simulation of combat scenarios over multiple sessions. Self-reported PTSD symptoms of the soldiers were greatly diminished compared to pretreatment reports.[7] We probably don't ever want to be able to do what was done to Joel and David. But a bit of that technology is coming. Science is helping people remember, or at least remember with less dysfunction, rather than erasing memories altogether.

Notes

[1,2] Moore, B.E., & Fine, B.D., Eds. (1990). *Psychoanalytic Terms and Concepts*. New Haven, CT: American Psychoanalytic Association.

[3] Shapiro, F., & Vogelmann-Sine, S. (1994). Eye movement desensitization and reprocessing: Treating trauma and substance abuse. *Journal of Psychoactive Drugs, 26,* 379-391.

[4] Shapiro, F., & Forest, M.S. (1997). *EMDR: The Breakthrough Therapy for Overcoming Anxiety, Stress, and Trauma.* New York: BasicBooks.

[5] Solomon, R.M., & Shapiro, F. (2008). Potential mechanisms of change. *Journal of EMDR Practice and Research*, *2*, 315-325.

[6] De Silva, P., & Rachman, S. (1981). Is exposure a necessary condition for fear-reduction? *Behaviour Research and Therapy*, *19*, 227-232.

[7] Reger, G.M., Gahm, G.A. (2008). Virtual reality exposure therapy for active duty soldiers. *Journal of Clinical Psychology: In Session, 64,* 940–946.

PULP FICTION (1994) & GO (1999)

In this Act we have explored subjects like imagination, dreams, and painful memories. We wrap with a pair of movies that were sophomore efforts from influential directors on the rise. *Pulp Fiction* was Quentin Tarantino's hugely successful follow-up to *Reservoir Dogs* (1992), which put him on the map as the "in-your-face-so-deal-with-it" filmmaker of his generation. *Go* was Doug Liman's well-crafted follow-up to his break-out indie hit *Swingers* (1996). Tarantino and Liman used innovative techniques to tell their stories, and we will consider the psychological grounding of those techniques.

A Tarantino Classic and a Neo-Noir Starter Kit

Both *Pulp Fiction* and *Go* feature bevies of criminals and low-lifes (though *Pulp Fiction* goes way, *way* lower in that department- thank you very much, Zed and "The Gimp") played by quality ensemble casts. *Go* could be viewed as a *Pulp Fiction* starter kit - parents wanting to verse their kids in cinema history (there are some parents out there like that, right?) could use *Go* as a warm-up exercise of sorts.

Each movie is set in Los Angeles (though *Go* heads to Vegas, baby!) and structured by a trio of intersecting story lines, including some overlapping scenes that give the audience different perspectives on the plot. For example, in *Go*, Ronna is hit by a car in a parking lot outside a night club- severely injuring her but saving her life from the wrath of Todd the drug dealer (who was about to introduce her to his semi-automatic). The intersected story of gay TV stars Adam and Zack later divulges that they were the ones who accidentally ran her over. In *Pulp Fiction* the overlaps are more fleeting, such as when we hear Ringo ask for a "garcon" as Jules and Vincent eat breakfast and discuss Jules' spiritual conversion at the diner. Or when the gunman in Brett's apartment listens to Jules' recitation of Ezekiel 25:17 before emerging from the bathroom with hand cannon blazing.

Both movies have drug over-dose scenes, though the one in *Pulp Fiction*, of course, is much more intense. Both start and end with a diner sequence. *Pulp Fiction* opens with Ringo and Yolanda in a booth discussing the best practices in armed robbery. The audience gets to know them a bit, but has to wait until the movie comes full circle to find out what happens to their hold-up attempt. In *Go*, Liman uses a device Hitchcock famously employed in *Notorious* (1946)- refusing to reveal who Claire is eating (and flirting) with; the audience has to wait until the end to learn his identity. Finally, Tarantino and Liman share a penchant for witty banter sprinkled with plenty of pop culture references: Big Macs, Obi-Wan Kenobi, Marilyn Monroe, "The Family Circle," etc.

PULP FICTION

Directed by
Quentin Tarantino

Cast
John Travolta as Vincent Vega, Samuel L. Jackson as Jules Winnfield, Bruce Willis as Butch Coolidge, Tim Roth as Pumpkin/Ringo, Amanda Plummer as Honey Bunny/Yolanda, Uma Thurman as Mia Wallace, Christopher Walken as Captain Koons, Quentin Tarantino as Jimmie Dimmick

Oscar Wins
Best Writing, Screenplay Written Directly for the Screen

Oscar Nominations
Best Picture
Best Actor in a Leading Role (John Travolta)
Best Actor in a Supporting Role (Samuel L. Jackson)
Best Actress in a Supporting Role (Uma Thurman)
Best Director
Best Film Editing

Golden Globe Wins
Best Screenplay – Motion Picture

Metascore: 94

Altered Perceptions

By breaking the mold of traditional, sequential story-telling, both Tarantino and Liman created films that illustrate psychological ideas related to perception and memory. In each movie characters are introduced in the opening moments, and then the stories circle around to them at the end. How the audience views the characters and situations is altered by the intervening events. This is certainly true in *Go*, when at the outset the mysterious figure seems likable (at least to Claire), but Todd turns out to be quite the thug.

With implicit memory, previous experiences aid in the performance of a task without conscious awareness of these experiences.[1] In this case the "previous experiences" would be events between the opening scene and the ending. When we watch movies we are not passively absorbing the sights and sounds because perception is not the passive receipt of signals. Rather, our perceptions are shaped by learning, memory, and expectation. Liman and Tarantino built a lot of priming into their films which elevates the statuses of their low-life characters to charismatic protagonists, and even sympathetic heroes.

> **Go**
>
> **Directed by**
> Doug Liman
>
> **Cast**
> Sarah Polley as Ronna Martin, Scott Wolf as Adam, Jay Mohr as Zack, Katie Holmes as Claire Montgomery, Desmond Askew as Simon Baines, William Fichtner as Burke
>
> **Metascore: 72**

Priming is an implicit memory effect in which exposure to a stimulus alters a response to a subsequent stimulus. For instance, if someone reads a list of words including the word "string," and is later asked to complete a word starting with *str-*, there is a higher likelihood that he will answer "string" due to the priming. Another example is if someone sees a partial sketch that they are unable to identify (like of a ship) and are shown more of the sketch until they recognize it as ship, later they will identify the ship at an earlier stage than was possible for them the first time.[2] The characters in these movies are often embedded in banal activities, like talking about fast food. So when we reflect on the characters, we fill in positive attributes around the negative, like recalling the word "string" or the image of a ship. It helps that the audience can relate to the banal activities and even agree with some of the characters' opinions (haven't we all hated on "Family Circle" at some point?). The end result can be a disorienting experience for the audience- being drawn in by criminals and deviants. Tarantino and Liman could have stuck with just the most dreadful aspects of underworld life. But by leveraging implicit memory and priming, they formed bonds between the audience and their characters and embedded the movie-goer into their worlds. So all that dialogue about Whoppers and Amway served a psychological purpose.

Notes

[1] Schacter, D.L. (1987). Implicit memory: history and current status. *Journal of Experimental Psychology: Learning Memory, and Cognition, 13*, 501-518.

[2] Kolb, B., & Whishaw, I.Q. (2003). *Fundamentals of Human Neuropsychology, 5th edition* . Worth: Virginia.

CinemAnalysis

Act VI

BioFlicks:

Lifespan on Screen

E.T. THE EXTRA-TERRESTRIAL (1982) & HOW TO TRAIN YOUR DRAGON (2010)

So we have come to our final Act, in which we will explore how people progress through life- from childhood, to young adulthood, to the twilight years. We'll go chronologically, more or less, beginning with a pair of movies about how children relate with their parents (single parents, in this case). These movies work their magic by telling their own version of the *boy and his dog* story. Be sure to have a box of tissues on hand, because this double-feature will deliver some tearjerker moments.

Two Boys and Their "Dogs"

E.T. the Extra-Terrestrial is one of director Steven Spielberg's many classics. He tells the story of an alien (dubbed "ET") who comes to earth to explore and accidentally gets marooned near a suburban neighborhood. He makes his way into the home of Elliot, the middle of three children being raised by single-mom Mary. The relationship between the stressed-out Mary and her children is strained. But Elliot and his mother get closer, in large part because she comes to admire the tenacity with which Elliot protects ET from the horde of scientists who descend on their home to accost the alien.

How to Train Your Dragon is an animated film that deserves a place in the upper echelon of family films. The story revolves around a Viking boy named Hiccup, who lives in a village beset by dragons who raid it for livestock. Hiccup's father is the head honcho and alpha dragon slayer, Stoick the Vast. Stoick is a single father and he just doesn't get Hiccup, who is a clumsy warrior better suited for tinkering as a blacksmith. During a dragon raid, Hiccup manages to bag one of the most mysterious species of dragons, the "night furies." Since no one believes Hiccup, he has to

CinemAnalysis

> **E.T.: THE EXTRA-TERRESTRIAL**
>
> **Directed by**
> Steven Spielberg
>
> **Cast**
> Dee Wallace as Mary, Henry Thomas as Elliot, Peter Coyote as Keys, Robert MacNaughton as Michael, Drew Barrymore as Gertie
>
> **Oscar Wins**
> Best Effects, Sound Effects Editing
> Best Effects, Visual Effects
> Best Music, Original Score
> Best Sound
>
> **Oscar Nominations**
> Best Picture
> Best Director
> Best Writing, Screenplay Written Directly for the Screen
> Best Cinematography
> Best Film Editing
>
> **Golden Globe Wins**
> Best Original Score – Motion Picture
> Best Motion Picture – Drama
>
> **Metascore: 94**

go into the forest the next day for evidence of his trophy. What he finds is a wounded, kind creature that he decides to nurse back to health, rather than slay. The dragon, dubbed "Toothless," even allows his friend Hiccup to fly him. Of course, things go awry for the Vikings, but Hiccup and Toothless manage to save the day. In the process Stoick lets go of his hatred of dragons and his disappointment in Hiccup, and he starts to appreciate the considerable gifts his son has to offer.

Both movies feature thrilling scenes of flight (in *E.T.* the famous shot of the bicycle soaring across the moon and in *How to Train Your Dragon* Hiccup's first sortie atop Toothless). But the key strand of shared DNA across *E.T.* and *How to Train Your Dragon* is how a misunderstood, insecure boy grows in confidence through selflessness and the courage required to keep his "dog" hidden from malevolent forces. In both of these films, the relationship between boy and "dog" paves the way for a stronger bond between boy and single mother/father (and each boy also starts to connect more with siblings and peers).

Parenting Styles

We take for granted that when marriages break up kids are caught in the crossfire and can suffer emotional consequences. While the absence of Hiccup's mother is never explained in *How to Train Your Dragon*, a divorce has clearly taken place in *E.T.* Research indicates that marital dissolution can put kids through the emotional wringer. That said, individuals differ in how they respond to that adversity. Divorce actually benefits some children, negatively affects others temporarily, and pushes others on a long-term downward trajectory.[1] Both Hiccup and Eliot end up in good places by the end of their stories. They are both more confident, mature, and, well, heroic. In contrast to the hierarchy of a two-parent household, a single-parent household typically forgoes such an echelon structure; this permits working single parents to share household responsibility with their children, leading to a ramp up in maturity.[2] This certainly is on-display with Hiccup, who as an adolescent has become a blacksmith apprentice and helps to defend the village from a dragon attack (albeit with mixed results). Eliot is younger than Hiccup, but there is some evidence of his taking on more responsibility (like paying the pizza delivery guy curbside).

While children in divorced families are at increased risk for social, emotional, and behavioral problems, most emerge as well-functioning individuals. Inter-parental conflict is a huge risk factor; in fact "children adjust better in a harmonious single-parent

> **HOW TO TRAIN YOUR DRAGON**
>
> **Directed by**
> Dean Deblois & Chris Sanders
>
> **Cast**
> Jay Baruchel as Hiccup, Gerard Butler as Stoick, Craig Ferguson as Gobber, America Ferrera as Astrid, Jonah Hill as Snotlout, Christopher Mintz-Plasse as Fishlegs, T.J. Miller as Tuffnut, Kristen Wiig as Ruffnut
>
> **Oscar Nominations**
> Best Animated Feature Film of the Year
> Best Achievement in Music Written for Motion Pictures, Original Score
>
> **Metascore: 74**

household than in an acrimonious two-parent household".[3] So the fact that Eliot's father and Hiccup's mother are out of the picture could benefit the boys, to the degree that they had contentious relationships with Mary and Stoick, respectively.

An important protective factor for kids in dissolved families is authoritative parenting.[4] Baumrind[5] defined three parenting styles:

- authoritarian- defined by the harsh use of discipline; parents using this style often do not listen to their children's concerns, encourage disagreement, nor explain their decisions; this style leads to insecure children

- permissive- marked by warmth towards children but with few demands for initiative or achievement; discipline is lax or inconsistent with this style, which leads to immature children

- authoritative- combines firmness and affection; parents with this style are encouraging and communicate well in terms of goals and standards; they promote independent decision-making in their children, cultivating self-reliance and positive adjustment

Early in *How to Train Your Dragon*, Stoick exemplifies the authoritarian style with his "my-way-or-the-highway" attitude. At the outset of *E.T.*, Mary is stuck in a permissive style of parenting; she is so frazzled that she is largely disengaged from her children, who are often left to fend for themselves. Fortunately for Hiccup and Eliot, though, their parents shift towards the authoritative mode by the end of the stories. Stoick develops a belief in Hiccup (and Toothless) that enables him to let his son charge alone into harm's way. Mary doesn't play as active a role in Eliot's heroic ascension, but she also starts believing in him and his mission to help ET return home. These parents find a healthy balance between letting go and supporting, and are better able to communicate with their sons in ways that breeds trust and respect.

Notes

[1] Amato, P.R. (2000). The consequences of divorce for adults and children. *Journal of Marriage and Family, 62*, 1269-1287.

[2] Weiss, R.S. (2010). Growing up a little faster: The experience of growing up in a single-parent household. *Journal of Social Issues, 35*, 97-111.

[3,4] Hetherington, E.M., & Stanley-Hagan, M. (1999). The adjustment of children with divorced parents: A risk and resiliency perspective. *Journal of Child and Adolescent Psychiatry, 40*, 129-140.

[5] Baumrind, D. (1967). Child care practices anteceding three patterns of preschool behavior. *Genetic Psychology Monographs, 75*, 43-88.

WHERE THE WILD THINGS ARE (2009) & FERRIS BUELLER'S DAY OFF (1986)

This double feature includes boys of similar ages to Eliot from *E.T.* and Hiccup from *How to Train Your Dragon*. But whereas the previous chapter was largely about how the boys related to their single parents, now we'll explore other forces that shape affect development. Both films show success stories of boys learning to meet challenges they face as they mature.

Boys Will Be Boys

Where the Wild Things Are is an adaptation of Maurice Sendak's children's book by the same name. The film centers on a 9 year-old boy named Max who is sent to bed without his supper because of his unruly behavior. Max's conduct is not entirely without cause; he is troubled by his father's absence, his mother's new love interest, and his sister maturing and pulling away from him. In response to his punishment, Max runs away from home and magically travels to an island where he meets powerful, yet lonely monsters who declare him their new king. It soon becomes apparent that the monsters have their own set of emotional problems as they ask King Max to "keep out all the sadness." What the monsters want is also what Max wants because they all embody parts of him and his fragmented family. For example, the monster Carol personifies the aggressive part of Max, Judith seems to be Max's sister, and the two owls appear to be his sister's

> **WHERE THE WILD THINGS ARE**
>
> **Directed by**
> Spike Jonze
>
> **Cast**
> Max Records as Max, Pepita Emmerichs as Claire, Catherine Keener as Mom, Mark Ruffalo as The Boyfriend, James Ganolfini as Carol, Catherine O'Hara as Judith, Forest Whitaker as Ira, Spike Jonze as Bob/Terry
>
> **Metascore: 71**

strange and confusing friends. Eventually Max and the monsters make peace with each other, and he sails back to the real world where his mother is waiting for him (with a supper that is still hot).

Ferris Bueller's Day Off is the story of "one man's struggle to take it easy." The protagonist is Ferris, a high-schooler who has come down with a bad case of senior-itus. Despite the fact that he can't afford any more absences, he convinces his best friend, Cameron, and girlfriend, Sloane, to blow off school and "borrow" Cameron's dad's restored Ferrari so that they can see the sights in downtown Chicago. In the face of a jealous sister, an angry and determined principal, and some very close calls, Ferris and his friends manage to have a blast without getting caught.

These movies look at boyhood from varying angles. They show a 9 year-old and an 18 year-old working out their respective developmental challenges without the support of adults. Ferris helps his friend Cameron loosen up from all the stressors of finishing high school by breaking the rules, living dangerously, and having fun with just enough time to pick up the pieces (well, most of them) to not get caught. Max uses fantasy, adventure, and play to work out his loneliness and anger.

The Quarter-Life Crisis

At its core, parenting is loving and nurturing a child so that he or she is capable of living a happy and fulfilling life, autonomous from parents. Both of these films tell stories of boys flying solo from their parents on their journeys towards independence. Max's journey is largely about reconciling the swirl of emotions he's experiencing (resentment, anxiety, excitement). Usually parents play a big role in helping kids learn to regulate emotions. Ferris, being older, is fairly detached from his parents, who mostly serve as foils for his shenanigans. Max is apart from his mother for the bulk of the story, leaving him with his imagination.

Verbal communication begins early in a child's life. But the younger the child, the more central play is to learning (play can speak much louder than words).[1] Max uses fantasy (pretend play) to work out his feelings of sadness, isolation, resentment, and anger. In this film adaptation, Max is 9 years old and is transitioning from a play-centered mentality into more verbal communication. At the most primitive state, Max and the monsters throw dirt balls, smash things, and build a fort. This play acts out notions of competition, strength, and having a sense of safety and belonging. He roars at the monsters, declaring he has "a sadness shield that keeps out all the sadness!" Such statements are a hybrid of pretend play and verbal communication. At other times he converses with his monsters, like when Judith says, "Happiness isn't always the best way to be happy." If Max saw a therapist, treatment would likely be the same kind of combination of play and verbal processing. The therapist might ask Max to draw some of his feelings or ask questions like, "If your anger was a monster, what would it look like? What would he say? Would he be a good monster, bad monster, or a little bit of both? How can he be your friend and you be king over him, instead of the other way around?" When children are prompted by parents to use pretend play they later become more skilled at emotional regulation.[2] Parents can help their children with emotional regulation with tactics such as talking about their own feelings, teaching positive self-talk, and coaching how to identify

> **FERRIS BUELLER'S DAY OFF**
>
> **Directed by**
> John Hughes
>
> **Cast**
> Matthew Broderick as Ferris Bueller, Alan Ruck as Cameron Frye, Mia Sara as Sloane Peterson, Jeffery Jones as Ed Rooney, Jennifer Grey as Jeanie Bueller
>
> **Metascore: 60**

elevating tension.[3]

    Ferris, Cameron, and Sloane may not be wrenched with the same heavy emotions as Max, but they are working out common adolescent challenges like identity formation, rebellion, anxiety about the future, and risk-taking. Facing these challenges is necessary for a young adult to individuate, form meaningful intimate relationships, and contribute unique qualities to society.[4] Necessary as it is, many young adults begin this "quarter life crisis" quite ungracefully and with associated consequences for risky behavior. We may not agree with the ethics of skipping school, lying, or stealing a car, but this story shows how an overzealous adult like the principal is clearly the villain and may deserve some insubordination in his ranks. The task for the three friends is to rebel against the parts of authority that are corrupt (such as the principal's oppressiveness or maniacal pleasure he would take in not graduating Ferris) while also retaining virtues that are congruent with their world view (like friendship, loyalty, and the sense of adventure).

    Actually, a lot of typical adolescent behaviors inherently involve risk, such as sports, travel, art, and making new friends.[5] Cameron is the most changed from the process because as much as he overshot his rebellion from his father, ultimately he realizes that he needs to stand up to him and "have a chat with the old man." Teens often have to experience undesirable consequences of their actions before they can learn the appropriate mixture of rebellion and harmony. Ferris' parents are extremely gullible and oblivious to his antics. But parents of adolescents can help their kids navigate risk for optimal benefit by talking about how to evaluate risk and anticipate consequences, as well as providing alternatives to risky activities. Also, parents can share their own histories of risk-taking and experimenting and be positive role-models by attending to their current patterns of risk-taking; teenagers are watching and imitating, whether they acknowledge it or not.[6]

Notes

[1] Anderson-McNamee, J., & Bailey, S. (2010). *The Importance of play in early childhood development*. Bozeman, MT: Montana State University Extension.

[2] Galyer, K.T. & Evans, I.M. (2006) Pretend Play and the Development of Emotion Regulation in Preschool Children. *Early Child Development and Care, 166*, 93-108.

[3] Friedberg, R.D. & McClure, J.M. (2002). *Clinical Practice of Cognitive Therapy with Children and Adolescents: the Nuts and Bolts.* New York: Guilford.

[4] Simpson, R.A. (2011). *Ten Tasks of Adolescent Development.* Retrieved from http://hrweb.mit.edu/worklife/raising-teens/ten-tasks.html

[5,6] Ponton, L.E. (1997). *The Romance of Risk: Why Teenagers Do the Things They Do.* New York: Basic.

(500) Days of Summer (2009) & Annie Hall (1977)

Having touched on childhood the last two chapters, it's time to grow up. The next stage of life is young adulthood, which is where we find the main characters in the first entry in this double-feature. Its partner is about mid-life characters, but the movies share enough parallels for them to have been separated at birth.

Post-Modern Romantic Comedies

Annie Hall is one of the best romantic comedies ever made, in large part because Woody Allen subverted the form in many ways (including punting the Hollywood happy ending). *Annie Hall* combines disparate styles and elements, such as animation and breaking the 4th wall (a great scene in which protagonist Alvy calls out an annoying fellow moviegoer by pulling in philosopher Marshall McLuhan himself).

(500) Days of Summer is a direct descendant of *Annie Hall*. Among the many shared strands of cinematic, post-modern DNA are jumping time cuts (that take the audience back and forth and back again across the romance of Tom and Summer), a musical number bursting out in downtown Los Angeles (to Hall and Oates' "You Make My Dreams," no less), a fleeting break of the 4th wall, and an inspired split-screen sequence comparing our hero Tom's expectations with heart-breaking reality. The movie also

> **(500) Days of Summer**
>
> **Directed by**
> Marc Webb
>
> **Cast**
> Joseph Gordon-Levitt as Tom, Zooey Deschanel as Summer, Geoffrey Arend as McKenzie, Chloë Grace Moretz as Rachel, Matthew Gray Gubler as Paul, Clark Gregg as Vance, Minka Kelly as Autumn
>
> **Metascore: 76**

makes the post-modern move of announcing that it is *not* a love story (or is it?). Finally, *(500) Days of Summer* took some stabs at retro fashion statements (like sweater vests) ala the trend-setting style of *Annie Hall* (she looked pretty cool in that vest and tie get-up).

As in *Annie Hall*, the boy in *(500) Days of Summer* doesn't get the girl (or does he?). Most importantly, both Alvy and Tom are nudged along in their lives by their star-crossed relationships with Annie and Summer, respectively. As Alvy puts it, we have relationships, as crazy as they can be, because we "need the eggs." And Tom needed Summer to get his proverbial ball bouncing in rhythm.

All The World's a (Developmental) Stage

These two movies emphasize the importance of relationships, especially of the romantic kind, in personal development. Renowned psychologist Erik Erikson wrote about 8 life stages, each of which is partly defined by a conflict to be resolved in order for growth to occur (1980). Tom and Summer of *(500) Days of Summer* would be in stage 6, or Young Adulthood, which involves the conflict between intimacy/solidarity (finding meaningful relationships) and isolation. Tom yearns for attachment and feels strongly that Summer will provide

ANNIE HALL

Directed by
Woody Allen

Cast
Woody Allen as Alvy Singer, Diane Keaton as Annie Hall, Tony Roberts as Rob, Carol Kane as Allison, Paul Simon as Tony Lacy, Shelly Duvall as Pam

Oscar Wins
Best Picture
Best Actress in a Leading Role (Diane Keaton)
Best Director
Best Writing, Screenplay Written Directly for the Screen

Oscar Nominations
Best Actor in a Leading Role (Woody Allen)

Metascore: N/A

him with that. Through most of the story Summer does not think that she wants that until she finds someone (other than Tom) who fills that previously undetected void. Erikson also proposed that successful resolution of the conflict at each stage results in the development of a virtue.[1] The resulting virtue for stage 6, Young Adulthood? *Love*. Hmmm . . . maybe this movie is a love story after all.

Alvy of *Annie Hall* is a bit older and is in stage 7, or Middle Adulthood. For Erikson, the conflict at this stage is between generativity and self-absorption/stagnation; it's about putting down roots with a family and creating stability and worth. The virtue to be attained at this stage is *care*[2], and the risk is the mid-life crisis, which Alvy exemplifies with his insecurities (as opposed to, say, buying a sports car). Tom seems to be on his way through stage 6 when fate smiles on him in the final moments of *(500) Days of Summer*. Alvy's direction is less clear, but he acknowledges how much better off he was for having known Annie, who inadvertently pushed him out of his various comfort zones along the way. But he may be working through Middle Adulthood for a while.

Notes

[1,2] Erikson, E.H. (1980). *Identity and the life cycle*. New York: Norton.

Before Sunrise (1995), Before Sunset (2004), & Before Midnight (2013)

This chapter represents a break in form, with a triple-feature instead of a double-feature. These three movies, all directed by Richard Linklater and starring Ethan Hawke and Julie Delpy, make for a story arc from young adulthood into the full throes of middle adulthood. Each of these films can stand alone, but the narratives deepen greatly when watched as a trilogy 18 years in the making.

Before and After

In *Before Sunrise*, Jesse and Celine are twenty-somethings who have a chance encounter while riding a train through Europe. Over the course of just a few hours, they both become aware of a chemistry between them. Jessie convinces Celine to delay her return home to Paris and instead get off the train with him in Vienna as he kills time before his flight back to the U.S. The film takes place over the course of one night as their deep and personal conversation jumps from topic to topic and grows increasingly captivating. Though they are falling in love, they have to confront the impossibility of being together and yet the impossibility of letting go. At the last moments of their time together, they decide to meet again at the same train station 6 months later. The audience is left to wonder whether each will follow through.

> **Before Sunrise**
>
> **Directed by**
> Richard Linklater
>
> **Cast**
> Ethan Hawke as Jesse, Julie Delpy as Céline
>
> **Metascore: 77**

Before Sunset takes place 9 years later, when Jesse is on the last stop of a book tour in Paris and, of course, he runs into Celine. The two talk again about their love for each other back then, and (as they become more vulnerable) as it still exists. Now the challenge of their being together doesn't just lie in geographic distance, but because Jessie has a wife and a child back home. In the last moments of the film, Jesse is procrastinating going to the airport and Celine says, "You are going to miss your flight," to which Jesse replies "I know."

Before Midnight takes place another 9 years later. Jesse decided to stay with Celine and they are now in the 9th year of their relationship. Although the couple still has the original spark of connection, there is also an added layer of tension between them. Jesse confesses that because of his decision to be with Celine, he feels he is neglecting his now teenage son who lives with ex-wife back in the U.S. Celine makes reference to being uncomfortable with the autobiographical novel Jesse wrote; while their story once felt so romantic, now it seems too intimate to be shared with the world. This third installment is at times inspiring, but also sad. As hard as the choice is to be together, the decision to stay together is ongoing and more complex.

> **BEFORE SUNSET**
>
> **Directed by**
> Richard Linklater
>
> **Cast**
> Ethan Hawke as Jesse, Julie Delpy as Céline
>
> **Oscar Nominations**
> Best Writing, Adapted Screenplay
>
> **Metascore: 90**

Because these stories take place and were made at 9-year intervals, the characters and actors both mature in terms of temperaments, minds, and bodies. Jesse and Celine grapple with some similar questions across the films but arrive at different answers. Jesse, once so cynical, becomes more optimistic, while Celine goes in the opposite direction. In each installment it is clear the couple's connection is deep and beautiful and yet being together proves to be exceedingly difficulty. All along the way, we root for them to overcome the challenges.

Sometimes Hot, Sometimes Heavy

This trilogy is a powerful case study of how romantic love develops over the lifespan and how individuals don't just wrestle with what values to hold, but also how to balance and prioritize them. Most everyone wants a strong and permanent connection with their romantic partner, but how important is this when it is pitted against career or rearing children? In *Before Midnight*, Jesse is torn between his obligation as a father and his love for Celine. What makes his situation so agonizing is that he might, at times, have to pick one over the other. Choosing his son and living in the States might be seen as a rejection by Celine.

Much of the work in psychotherapy involves helping individuals make peace with desires that are at odds. We tend to want to have it all but deep down we know that having everything is impossible. Successful long-term relationships require compatible values, as well as compatible priorities within the framework of these values. It is disheartening to encounter something that is good and beautiful, such as the connection Jesse and Celine have, yet recognize that having it requires letting go of other good or desirable things like being the best kind of father, having a cherished location, or career goals.

> **BEFORE MIDNIGHT**
>
> **Directed by**
> Richard Linklater
>
> **Cast**
> Ethan Hawke as Jesse, Julie Delpy as Céline, Seamus Davey-Ftizpatrick as Hank
>
> **Oscar Nominations**
> Best Writing, Adapted Screenplay
>
> **Metascore: 94**

Successful therapy often gets at the heart of ambivalence- understanding it, accepting it, and making the best and often painful choices when negotiating desires. A tactic for a family therapist is to think of the family or couple as a unit that is made of different parts. Promoting healthy changes for the family as a whole might have painful consequences for a particular member. Likewise, what might be good for an individual in an overall sense might be painful to them in some particular domain or for a period of time.[1] For this reason, family therapy entails some exceedingly difficult decisions if it hopes to promote overall welfare for the family. Were Jesse and Celine to work with a therapist, all would need to maintain a strong sense of personal values, appreciation for the complexity of balancing those values, and a long-term vision of welfare to successfully traverse the daunting and beautiful world that they share.

Notes

[1] Zygmond, M.J., & Boorhem, H. (1989). Ethical decision making in family therapy. *Family Process, 28*, 269-280.

Bridesmaids (2011) & Jerry Maguire (1996)

This double feature is about something that is actually rather nebulous in psychology- the mid-life crisis. Although most of us can readily spot a mid-life crisis when we see it, the causes and dynamics are not always clear. One thing is for sure, *Bridesmaids* and *Jerry Maguire* can make you feel better in two ways. First, they can point out how much worse your life could be. Second, they show how it's possible to reclaim your mojo.

Rock Bottom

Bridesmaids isn't about a wedding. It isn't really about the build-up to a wedding, either. It's about someone who has hit rock bottom and is trying to climb out of the pit. That someone is Annie, a middle-aged pastry chef who lost her bakery during the Great Recession. She's living with a couple of hapless (though highly amusing) siblings from England. She fools around with a total jerk. And she's in danger of losing her best friend, Lillian, not to her husband-to-be, but rather to Helen, a Stepford wife competing to be Lillian's best friend and maid of honor. By story's end Annie hasn't put her life back together, but she is on her way. The story's restraint along these lines is refreshing. For example, rather than Annie triumphantly getting her bakery back, we instead get a

---

BRIDESMAIDS

Directed by
Paul Feig

Cast
Kristen Wiig as Annie, Rose Byrne as Helen, Maya Rudolph as Lillian, Michael Hitchcock as Don Cholodecki, Rebel Wilson as Brynn, Melissa McCarthy as Megan, Jon Hamm as Ted, Chris O'Dowd as Rhodes

Oscar Nominations
Best Performance by an Actress in a Supporting Role (Melissa McCarthy)
Best Writing, Original Screenplay

Metascore: 75

scene in which she plaintively decorates a cupcake, showing that she still has chops. She meets a nice guy, Nathan, who doesn't sweep her off her feet, but gives their budding relationship a chance.

Jerry Maguire is also about someone bottoming out, but with a steeper story arc. At the outset, hot shot sports agent Jerry is on top of the world. Money. Juice. Hot fiancée. But he's troubled by how shaky his moral compass has become. His attempt to straighten that compass gets him fired, so he also loses his money, juice, hot fiancée, etc. Fortunately, he finds Dorothy, a single mom with whom he starts a new agency and a romance. The rest of the story is about Jerry putting his life back together. He's helped by the relationship with his only client, Rod, a diva NFL wide receiver but also a role model family man. Incidentally, Annie also gets a boost from a flamboyant friend, the riotous Megan. By story's end Jerry is in better shape than Annie. He's married to Dorothy, their new agency is on a roll, and he's done it all with a stabilized moral compass.

Crisis Management

Hitting the skids in middle age can look like desperate attempts to reclaim youth (think new sports car, trophy wife, and cosmetic surgery). But it can also result in serious mental health problems. Research has confirmed that acute work-related stress (like what Annie and Terry endure) contributes to psychological disorders like depression.[1] Depression is one of the most prevalent forms of psychopathology, afflicting approximately 20 to 25% of women and 10 to 17% of men within their lifetime.[2] The traditional view was that the relationship between life stress and depression was unidirectional. This seems intuitive- if someone loses her livelihood she could go into a tailspin, the stress causing depression. This was called the stress exposure model, proposing that stressful life events significantly increase a person's susceptibility to depression.[3]

But how would we account for the fact that Annie and Jerry become even bigger train wrecks as their stories unfold? Jerry gets fired, *then* loses a hugely important client, *then* breaks up with his fiancée, *then* rushes into a marriage with Dorothy, and so on. Annie loses her business, *then* moves in with two morons, *then* gets romantically involved with a jerk, *then* sparks a rivalry with Helen, *then* can't see what a good thing she has going with Nathan, and so on. They both are melodrama magnets.

> **JERRY MAGUIRE**
>
> **Directed by**
> Cameron Crowe
>
> **Cast**
> Tom Cruise as Jerry Maguire, Cuba Gooding Jr. as Rod Tidwell, Renee Zellweger as Dorothy Boyd, Kelly Preston as Avery Bishop, Jerry O'Connell as Frank Cushman
>
> **Oscar Wins**
> Best Actor in a Supporting Role (Cuba Gooding Jr.)
>
> **Oscar Nominations**
> Best Picture
> Best Actor in a Leading Role (Tom Cruise)
> Best Film Editing
> Best Writing, Screenplay Written Directly for the Screen
>
> **Golden Globe Wins**
> Best Performance by an Actor in a Motion Picture – Comedy/Musical (Tom Cruise)
>
> **Metascore: 77**

Newer thinking about life stress and depression accounts for the bi-directional nature between the two. Individuals who are depressed report higher rates of stressful life events, especially those that have occurred in part because of the person's traits and how they navigate interpersonal interactions. Stress generation refers to the role of the individual as an active contributor, rather than a passive player, in his or her environment.[4] Research has substantiated the melodrama magnet idea, showing that depression plays an active role in generating the very stresses that place individuals at heightened risk for future depression.[5] The result is a downward spiral.

What is it about Annie or Jerry that draws trouble into their already troubled lives? Some of the factors that have been explored are dysfunctional attitudes, ruminating on thoughts, low self-confidence, negative feedback-seeking, blame maintenance, and interpersonal conflict avoidance.[6] Applying this list to Annie and Jerry, it's hard to know where to begin. Jerry has that always intriguing mix of egotism (the hotshot deal closer) and insecurity (am I really accomplishing anything of worth?). His fear of intimacy flows into conflict avoidance that almost derails his relationship with Dorothy- only after they have it out do they reconcile. Annie's fear of intimacy drives her from Nathan and draws her into a dysfunctional relationship. Though she and Lillian have a tremendous bond, she is so insecure with it that she allows Helen to get inside her head. And while she clearly has a ton of talent as a pastry chef, she lacks the confidence to give her career another go.

While neither Jerry nor Annie seek help from a mental health professional, both are at better places by stories' ends. They benefited from some good fortune, namely supportive friends and healthy romances coming into their lives. But they also made some good choices, so they weren't just at the mercy of luck. The result is that both got on an upward spiral (not all spirals are bad).

Notes

[1] Tennant, C. (2001). Work-related stress and depressive disorders. *Journal of Psychosomatic Research, 51*, 697-704.

[2] Levinson D.F. (2006). The genetics of depression: A review. *Biological Psychiatry, 60*, 84–92.

[3,5,6] Liu, R.T., & Alloy, L.B. (2010). Stress generation in depression: A systematic review of the empirical literature and recommendations for future study. *Clinical Psychology Review, 30*, 582-593.

[4] Hammen, C. (2006). Stress generation in depression: Reflections on

origins, research, and future directions. *Journal of Clinical Psychology, 62*, 1065-1082.

About Schmidt (2002) & The Visitor (2007)

In Act VI we started with childhood, moved up to young adulthood, and then on to mid-life. Naturally, we close this act (and this book) with a pair of films about the twilight years. These movies point out that even when a life is winding down, sometimes the journey just keeps on going.

New Tricks for Old Dogs

The central character of *The Visitor* is Walter, a widowed economics professor living a rather solitary existence. He begrudgingly travels to New York City to attend an academic conference, only to find living in his old apartment a young unmarried couple who rented it from a swindler. The couple are illegal immigrants- Tarek, a Syrian djembe player, and Zainab, a Senegalese jewelry designer. Realizing that Tarek and Zainab aren't really squatters, Walter allows them to stay and friendships slowly develop. Tarek teaches Walter to play the djembe (a drum). After a jam session at a drum circle in Central Park, Tarek is detained after police mistakenly think he jumped a subway turnstile. Tarek's mother, Mouna, unexpectedly arrives from her home in Michigan when she is unable to

> **About Schmidt**
>
> **Directed by**
> Alexander Payne
>
> **Cast**
> Jack Nicholson as Warren Schmidt, Kathy Bates as Roberta Schmidt, Hope Davis as Jeannie Schmidt, Dermot Mulroney Randall Hertzel, June Squibb as Helen Schmidt
>
> **Oscar Nominations**
> Best Actor in a Leading Role (Jack Nicholson)
> Best Actress in a Supporting Role (Kathy Bates)
>
> **Golden Globe Wins**
> Best Performance by an Actor in a Motion Picture – Drama (Jack Nicholson)
> Best Screenplay - Motion Picture
>
> **Metascore: 85**

contact him. Because she also is an illegal immigrant, she cannot risk visiting Tarek at the detention center. She and Walter develop a friendship; he treats her to *The Phantom of the Opera* after she mentions her love for the original cast recording Tarek sent her as a gift. When Tarek is abruptly deported to Syria, Mouna decides she must also return permanently. On their final night, Mouna joins Walter for an affectionate embrace in bed. Walter sees her off at the airport the next day. The film's final, lengthy shot is of Walter passionately playing the djembe on a subway platform.

In the opening moments of *About Schmidt*, Warren Schmidt retires as an actuary in Omaha, Nebraska. Schmidt finds post-career life difficult, feeling useless. He sees a television advertisement about a foster program for African children and decides to sponsor a child. Soon after he receives a package with a photo of his foster child, a small Tanzanian boy named Ndugu, to whom he writes a series of letters (that are serious to him, but hilarious to the audience). Helen, his wife, suddenly dies from a blood clot in her brain. Friends arrive, along with Jeannie, his only daughter, and her fiancé, Randall. Schmidt feels that Jeannie can do better than Randall, a waterbed salesman, and later decides to road trip in his new Winnebago to convince her to break up with him. He visits places from his past, including his hometown and college campus. Upon arriving in Denver, where Jeannie and Randall are to marry, he fails in his mission to torpedo the nuptials. He attends the wedding and, under the influence of painkillers taken because he threw out his back on one of Randall's waterbeds, delivers a thoughtful speech at the reception, hiding his disapproval. Before leaving Denver, Schmidt writes a letter to Ndugu in which he laments that he will soon be dead, that his life has made no difference to anyone, and that eventually it will be as if he has never existed at all. But when he gets home he finds a letter from Tanzania, written by a nun who conveys that Ndugu is illiterate but deeply appreciates Schmidt's letters and financial support. The letter includes a painting drawn by Ndugu, depicting large and small smiling stick figures, holding hands under the sun. The film's final shot is Schmidt weeping in delight.

The Rocking Chair Test

The eighth of Erik Erikson's life stages is Mature Age, marked by the conflict between integrity and disgust/despair. Think of this stage as having the "rocking chair" test in which a person in the twilight takes stock of his or her life. The virtue that results from resolving the conflict at this stage is wisdom. But some feel that they fail this test and have regrets and frustration about how their lives unfolded. The despair that Erikson described can manifest in many ways, such as anxiety about facing the end of life, contempt of particular institutions or people, and dissatisfaction with one's own self.[1] Jungian psychoanalyst James Hollis wrote that "death is only one way of dying; living partially, living fearfully, is our more common, daily collusion with death (2009, p. 92)."

Walter's Mature Age conflict clearly swings towards the disgust/despair end of the continuum at the outset of *The Visitor*. He is listless, both professionally and personally. But he is brought back to life by his new-found friendships, and by being needed by someone (both Tarek and Mouna). In addition, Tarek gives Walter the gift of

> **THE VISITOR**
>
> **Directed by**
> Thomas McCarthy
>
> **Cast**
> Richard Jenkins as Walter, Haaz Sleiman as Tarek, Danai Gurira as Zainab, Hiam Abbass as Mouna, Marian Seldes as Barbara
>
> **Oscar Nominations**
> Best Performance by an Actor in a Leading Role (Richard Jenkins)
>
> **Metascore: 79**

the djembe, which provides Walter a soul-stirring creative outlet. Although he is alone again at the end of the story, Walter certainly has shifted away from disgust/despair towards integrity.

Schmidt is dealing with a huge dose of disgust/despair in his Mature Age. But like Walter, Schmidt steps back from the abyss of disgust/despair with the help of relationships. Just as Walter got a burst of energy from making a different to Tarek and Mouna, Schmidt is rejuvenated by what he has done for Ndugu.

How realistic are the comeback tales of Walter and Schmidt? James Hollis takes an optimistic view of the prospects for end-of-life change. "The second half of life is a summons to the life of the spirit, namely, to ask, and answer for ourselves, uniquely, separately, *what matters most*."[2] Hollis would probably argue that Walter and Schmidt needed to be knocked around during the Mature Age. "To be defeated by ever-larger things is indeed our task, for that means we are growing, growing, growing."[3] In the final, poignant images from *The Visitor* and *About Schmidt*- Walter playing the drum and Schmidt weeping with joy- show men who indeed have grown.

And ... that's a wrap.

Okay, it's not quite a wrap yet. We'll continue pondering movies, dreaming up double features, and connecting them to psychology (that's a tap we just can't turn off). We invite you to do the same. Please share your thoughts with us. We'd relish the conversation.

There ... now it's a wrap.

Notes

[1] Erikson, E.H. (1980). *Identity and the life cycle.* New York: Norton.

[2,3] Hollis, J. (2009). *What matters most: Living a more considered life.* New York: Gotham.

CinemAnalysis

CinemAnalysis